D1745469

Emil Schulthess    China

*for Bruna*

Emil Schulthess

# China

A Studio Book    The Viking Press · New York

© Text 1966, Artemis Verlags-AG, Zurich and Stuttgart
© Illustrations 1966, Emil Schulthess
© English translation, text and captions, 1966, Wm. Collins Sons and Co. Ltd., London

Published in 1966 by The Viking Press, Inc.,
625 Madison Avenue, New York, N.Y. 10022

Library of Congress catalog card number: 66-23827
Translation: Text by Michael Heron and captions by Victor Andersen

Printed in Switzerland: Illustrations, gravure, by Imago, Zurich
Text, letterpress, by Stämpfli, Berne
Paper by Papierfabrik An der Sihl, Zurich
Binding by Stämpfli, Berne
Design by Emil Schulthess

# Foreword

Any foreigner travelling in the "Middle Kingdom", even though only parts of it are accessible, is deeply impressed by its immensity, the extraordinary variety of scenery, and even more by the evidences of its cultural heritage.

The face of China is marked by contrasts. What a tremendous difference there is between the densely populated lowlands with their endless rice paddies in the delta of the Yangtze, and the solitary deserts of Sinkiang and Inner Mongolia; between the desolate mountain ranges of West China and fertile, industrialized Manchuria in the north-east; between the bare, austere loess region on the middle reaches of the Yellow River and the tropical shores of the south-east coast. And how different are the people who have inhabited these parts of the country for thousands of years, how inconceivable the wealth that continually arose and disappeared in the course of the ages! Obviously one of the main concerns of this book is to weave what is going on in China today into this larger context.

In China the interactions between natural and cultural geography, and natural and human history, loom particularly large. They are already known to us—at least at second-hand—from early Chinese literature and landscape painting, but they confront us with immediate impact in the present book of photographs by Emil Schulthess. The better understanding of this country that the new book gives will also be a vital experience for the discerning observer. Perhaps, in such a complicated country as China, the incorruptible photograph most readily provides the language that leads to a better understanding of the problems of its civilization so rich in cultural tradition? China must be measured by other standards than those normally used in the rest of the world. The contrasts of its landscape and its climate are just as extreme as the oscillations of its history, which is many thousands of years old. That these continually lead to major ideological tensions is just being proved to us again today.

Nowadays there is no lack of publications about China. But their authors seldom manage to communicate to the reader a really life-like picture of this country, mainly because of the astonishing dimensions that have to be mastered. Although large parts of the country were also closed to Emil Schulthess, his documentation—which never loses its comprehensive general viewpoint, in spite of the particularities of his theme—fulfils our highest expectations. Undoubtedly his pictures, and the textual contributions of his co-authors Harry Hamm, Edgar Snow and Emil Egli, arouse new interest in and understanding for this original and many-faceted country of which we read and hear daily, and about which we still really know so little.

*Hans Keller*
*Swiss Ambassador in Peking*

# Landscape and Life in China    *by Emil Egli*

Asia is the continent of extremes, of superlatives. In this, the largest of all continental land masses, geology has erected the highest peaks in the world, the whitest, most resplendent thrones of religion. And the deepest depressions in the ocean bed lie off its coasts and archipelagoes; the third dimension of the earth's surface has been forced here into extremes of height and depth that have been beyond the reach of mankind until now. At the heart of this continent lie the regions of the earth most distant from the sea, as much as 3,000 miles from the coast, where the harsh elements of the steppes prevail. The peoples with the largest populations in the world, and with the densest agrarian populations, live in Asia. And since the forces of nature are constantly attacking these densely populated regions with all their might, Asia, especially in the south-east, is also the continent of the greatest natural catastrophes caused by typhoons, floods, droughts, earthquakes and volcanoes.

China forms part of this world. A giant state of continental dimensions (almost the size of Europe), it lies on the border of Asia and on the edge of the Pacific; formed, favoured, afflicted and threatened by both. "Dieu a donné au sol de la Chine un caractère particulier de grandeur", as that splendid documentary book *L'Empire Chinois* by Thomas Allom and Clément Pelle stated at the beginning of the last century. The spurs of the Central Asian mountain ranges divide up the country. Its rivers rise in the vastest massif in the world.

This encounter between the biggest continental mass and the largest ocean, with its far-reaching geographical effects, is one of the main reasons for the early development of a great culture here. This two-fold natural blessing may have fed that sense of living in a central situation, close to nature and created by her, which led to the conception of China as centre of the world. Although culturally active for thousands of years, and as grandiose in its technical public works as it was frugal in its everyday living, Chungkuo, the "Middle Kingdom", remained self-supporting and cut off from the world for a very long time. The name "China", for which there are at least two derivations, is not autochthonous. Sometimes it gave its name the poetic form Chung-hua, "Flower of the Middle". Only during the Manchu period (1644—1912) was it altered to Shia-pa Sheng, the "Eighteen provinces". After the collapse of the oldest monarchy in the world in 1912, the young republic called itself Chung-hua min-kuo, and the "People's Republic of China", proclaimed in Peking on September 21, 1949, officially bears the name Chung-hua jen-min kung-ho-kuo, which is most directly translated by "Empire and people of the flowering country of the middle".

If we try to envisage the physical structure of south-east Asia in a way that will rationalise it, the first thing we see is a massive fan of mountain ranges opening out eastwards from the Central Asian highlands towards the China Sea: the highlands of north China swing north-east; the southern continuation of the Himalayan range flanks China in the south-west and in the central zone the straight and narrow Tsinling Shan runs from west to east like a great dividing line. Simultaneously the continent descends eastward in a series of steps to the border seas familiar from our schooldays. Each step of this giant stairway is somewhat sunk inward, i.e. towards the west.

The lowest step, on the edge of the continent runs through Manchuria, the Yellow Sea and the north Chinese lowlands to the south Chinese highlands, embracing their eastern half. This broad coastal strip, so vital to China, is characterised on the landward side by lowlands and basins: the Hwang Ho plain and the great highland depressions with the chaotic land-water network of the Tung-ting-hu and Poyang-hu lake regions.

The next higher, more central step is made up of the Kweichow and Szechwan highlands, together with the Red Basin, and of the Shensi and Shansi, which shelve systematically westward into Inner Mongolia with their northern continuation, the Great Chingan.

Lastly, the Tibetan plateau, framed by the Himalayas and the Kunlun Shan, forms the third step. It is the geological stronghold of the continent, the biggest ice region on the earth and the source of the most famous Chinese rivers, the Hwang Ho and the Yangtzekiang.

We must, of course, mention that yet another step—the lowest of all—is sunk in the sea. Only its raised eastern edge towers above the ocean, forming the looped garland of islands that is so distinctive on the map, while the lower part of the step forms the bed of the border seas, which lie off the coast like courtyards of water. The fore-courts of the Empire of the Middle are the South China Sea and part of the East China Sea.

Here we have the grandiose tectonic foundation of Chinese civilization: on the one hand the mountain ranges fanning out to the east, and on the other the monumental rocky stairway descending from the highland peaks to the bottom of the sea. Both encourage inhabitants of the land masses, which are so severely continental and discouraging to life, to turn towards the ocean, a sphere of influence that favours civilization. On the two central steps, between high plateau and border sea, flowered the Chinese culture of the middle empire.

This vastness of scale also characterises many other features of the geographical picture. To begin with, the play of the atmosphere is influenced. The first thing to note in a climatic survey is that China lies in the northern temperate zone and only its southern provinces touch the earth's tropical belt—Kwantung, Kwangei and the island of Hainan. In principle, therefore, it is dominated by the seasonal changes caused by the sun when it is high or low in the sky. But the contrast between summer and winter is intensified by the encounter of large areas of land and sea. Their difference in temperature—hot land, cold sea in summer; cold land, warm sea in winter—produces the well-known monsoon winds. (Monsoon is derived from the Arabic *mausim,* which means "season". However, the traditional view of monsoons has been complicated and varied by recent research, and agreement on the new theories has not yet been reached.)

Like Europe, China belongs to the belt of cyclonic winds, and the exchanges of air between land and sea, in other words its monsoons, are disturbed as a result; they lack the more classical form of the Indian monsoons: the Chinese monsoon is less rigid and less permanent in direction and duration. In more modern phraseology we now talk of the "cyclonic monsoon" of East Asia and, as always, of the vital exchange of air between land and sea. The meteorological phenomenon is characterised "in summer by damp masses of air coming from the sea with frequent, intense precipitations and in winter by originally dry continental cold air coming from Inner Asia" (Joachim Blüthgen). And because, as already shown, China climbs up in steps and does not, as in India, rise immediately behind the lowlands as a wall of 8,000 ft peaks, there is particularly close interchange between the Chinese coastal region and the interior of the continent.

The summer monsoon with its burden of water rolls far inland over plains, mountains and steps, and with each impetus envelops the mountains with foaming clouds. On the edge of the continent one of the atmosphere's greatest suction pumps is in action: this is the maritime tropical air from Ogasawa (the Bonin Islands) entering the country. The frontal zone reaches South China in May or June, bringing its cyclonic monsoon rains, and then travels inland and northwards. At this time there is a great reawakening of the whole of nature. The plant world feels the urge to grow and is liberated from the dust and suspended animation, and the lower animal kingdom of insects and worms, too, creeps out of its hiding-places. At one time Buddhist monks were forbidden to go on pilgrimages when the rainy season began, because it was almost impossible to set foot on the ground without killing something. For thousands of years, year after year, the earth has been softened for the plough. The annual rainfall in Hongkong is 85 in., of which 45 per cent falls in summer. Inland and northwards the rainfall decreases; Kiukiang has 59.84 in., Peking 24.4 in. In the north of the Great Plain four-fifths of the rainfall is concentrated in the three summer months (Kolb).

In spite of the sultriness of the maritime monsoon air, the rains modify the summer rise in temperature in South China. Canton, which lies on the latitude of the central Sahara (23° N), has a July mean of 82.4 °F. But the fact that the coastal towns of Central and North China have only slightly lower July temperatures than Canton—Shanghai 80.6 °F, Tientsin 79.7 °F—demonstrates the assault of the same tropical maritime air masses along the whole Chinese coast. Thus we find climatic conditions regionally dominated by the powerful air currents; for while the summer temperature does not actually increase from north to south, it does rise from the coast inland with the decreasing influence of the monsoon. For example, Wuhan (Hangkow), which lies on the latitude of Shanghai, but some 435 miles further inland, has a hottest month of 83.3 °F (Shanghai = 80.6 °F). And the merchants of that commercial city must certainly have been inspired by this foretaste of the inner Asian inferno when they spread the word that if the devil returned to hell from Hangkow in summer, he would wrap himself in his cloak.

In other words, with the rising summer sun, the maritime air with its cargo of clouds sails across the country and modifies the rise in temperature on the coastal strip at the time when it is becoming high. Without this annual rain, set in motion by the land-sea antithesis, an enlarged Gobi Desert might cover vast areas of China. The not infrequent catastrophic droughts, due to regional failure of the cyclonic monsoon rains, demonstrate the dependence on the elements of hundreds of millions of Chinese. The life-awakening and life-preserving response of the heavens, when fatally high temperatures threatened the countryside, must have obsessed these people very early on, and continued to do so. Their intellectual relationship with the heavens must have taken concrete form, and the Emperor pronounced his harvest prayer in the Temple of Heaven in Peking summer after summer for countless generations. "The path, the way", the Tao, primarily understood as the regular course of nature (Tao of the heavens), was a concept of Chinese philosophy from the time of Lao Tze, i.e. from the publication of the Tao Teh King, the work attributed to him. The world is in a continuous state of transformation. The idea of this transformation, the Tao, is the only constant. The principle of the cycle is eternal and unfathomable, it is supernatural. But the cycle is not fixed, it is not mechanically schematic. It has its death-dealing exceptions: not only the regional rain shortages, but also its attacks of typhoons which fall in the summer monsoon period, especially in its last phase. Generated in the equatorial air turbulence above the waters off New Guinea, the spiral eddies travel westwards, then curve parabolically to the northeast to strike against the Chinese islands and coastal strips. With almost inconceivable pressures reaching 200 kilograms per square metre of vertical surface, their "air-drills" pass through towns and plantations, leaving battlefields behind them. But the raging eddies also whip up the waters, the air's sister element. And with breakers such as scarcely any other storms can raise, ships, junks and jetties are destroyed; and the panic-spreading claws of tidal waves clutch at people's coastal properties. On August 2, 1922, a typhoon in the province of Kwangtun (Yen Yü-ti) claimed 70,000 dead and injured.

During the July—September typhoon quarter, three to four typhoons can be reckoned on. But they are distributed over wide areas and are by no means always destructive. They sometimes supplement the creative work of the monsoon. The typhoon is an itinerant ring of rain with an "eye", free of rain and storms, in the middle.

The great throbbing of the atmosphere also dominates the pulse of the rivers. Even the typhoon rains can cause local rises in the watercourses. But the summer monsoon brings lasting high water into the whole of the country's system. The Hwang Ho is world famous for its efforts to drag its mud-filled summer burden through the wide plains and for the catastrophic way in which it bursts its banks on hundreds of occasions. But the Yangtzekiang, too, where it is congested in its celebrated gorge through which it passes on emerging from the Red Basin, rises 98—163 ft. above its low winter level. The nature of the great rivers provided technical problems during the thousands of years of Chinese history and they still do so for modern China.

In Inner Asia, in China's hinterland, lies another sea: the great sandy Gobi Desert. It, too, is essentially a product of the continent's colossal dimensions, the remoteness from the coast of its inner regions. The Chinese call the Gobi Sha-mo, "Sea of sand", and it loads the winter monsoon, whose gigantic atmospheric conveyor belt runs from land to sea, with its cargo. The winter monsoon is the sand bearer, but also the bringer of cold.

Peking has a mean January temperature of 24 °F; Oporto, on the same latitude on the west coast of Europe, has 47.4 °F. And southern China, too, has surprising winter temperatures: 54.6 °F in Canton in January, as against 65.2 °F in Calcutta on the same latitude.

The reason for the cold Chinese winter lies in the Siberian winter, in the interior of the continent. A large area of barometric high pressure develops over north-east Asia with its January temperatures between −40° and −58 °F. And from this persistent and oppressive area of high cold the winds flow seawards. There are no protecting Himalayas behind northern China, only some modest highlands. From a north-westerly direction the icy Siberian flood of air invades the flat countryside of northern China, and only over the mountains of southern China is the cold wind modified. "In the northern parts of the Great Plain the rivers are already covered with ice in November. So are the shores of the Yellow Sea for 3 to 4 months. That is the time when the camel caravans from Mongolia cross the Nankow Pass with naturally frozen mutton, antelopes and pheasants. The vegetation dies or loses its leaves; tilling the soil is completely abandoned

during the winter. The cloudless sky further increases the local nightly fall in temperature in a countryside that lacks its mantle of vegetation. Icy dust storms sweep the country. Even on calm days, especially in the north-west, 'dry mist', the dust haze of Inner Asia, prevents good visibility. The natives wear thick, padded, winter clothing; the houses have their *kangs,* heated sleeping benches made of brick. Owing to the lack of wood the North Chinese were led to use coal as fuel much earlier than we were" (G. Wegener).

Air that flows in the direction of rising temperatures remains dry, however cold it is. Thus the flood of cold air whirls up the sands of Mongolia, scoops up immense dust cargoes from the billows of the Sha-mo and carries them over China's northern provinces. This has been going on for thousands of years, although the process was magnified in the Pleistocene the Ice Ages which were not so much actual Ice Ages in east Asia as a succession of Hot and Cold Ages. One of the earliest men, the so-called Peking man of northern China, had already evolved by this period. The air-borne sand stream, blowing from the Gobi Desert, was particularly active during the Cold Ages. The quantities of sand that were shovelled out of the vast desert basin during those millennia are inconceivable. In the process, the contrasts in temperature continually tore up and powdered new, bare rock.

The "rock mill" of the vast Asian interior was indefatigable in delivering material. It piled up as loess in the mountains of Shensi and Shansi, mingled with the river deposits of the Great Plain, got caught up like snow-drifts on the western side of the hill of Shantung and reached its sharply defined southern border on the straight east-west chain of the Tsinling-shan, although it did break through the gap between the latter and the Hwaiyang-san into the plain of the Yangtzekiang (which was its most southerly extension).

The loess masses of the combined Ice Ages reach thicknesses of as much as 1,000 ft. These geological sandstorms of continental proportions, which raged round the old original mountains of north China depositing their burden and sometimes completely covering the ancient rocky skeletons, must have been grandiose scenic dramas. But even today the yellow dust storms whirl annually through the countryside and sometimes even in the streets of Peking. The dust forces its way into houses and between men's teeth. It enshrouds the landscape in a pale, ghostly light. But there is an unmistakable smile on the face of the Chinese farmer, for the keenly anticipated new mineral consignment is fertilising his fields as far as Shantung (Kolb).

The word "loess" is of German origin and was introduced into technical literature by the sinologist von Richthofen. The Chinese call it *hwang-tu,* "yellow earth". The main watercourse in the loess territory is the Yellow River, the Hwang Ho. Along with its mud, it flows into the Yellow Sea, the Hwang-hai. The royal colour of old China, the holy colour too, was yellow. One of the Emperor's titles was *Hwang-ti,* "Yellow Lord". Is it pure coincidence that we are in the yellow race's central region?

The loess region is an exceptionally fertile one for the farmer for the loess has two natural advantages: not only is it extremely fine-grained, but it is also shot through with rifts and capillaries left by the vanished grass roots of past periods. As a result, loess soil has an extraordinary capacity for the reception and storage of water. The valuable sand, annually renewing the soil with a fine layer, is fertilised by the yearly irrigation when the sun is higher. Out of this great cycle of the sand- and water-bringing wind, this creative cosmic pulsation, arose that community which is one of the oldest contemporary civilizations.

Finally one should add that the old, worn rumps of China's mountain ranges were partly rejuvenated into sharper relief by subsequent folding processes. Thus, when the Yen-shan range was formed at the end of the geological middle ages and the later Alpine folding period, came the formation of the rifts and basins that seem as if they were made for the courses of the Chinese rivers and for the special loess deposits.

Once this strangely compounded geological and atmospheric event had taken place, the first consequence was an early and unusually populous civilization. During the third millennium, in the labyrinth of valleys of the loess country, arose the Neolithic Yang-shao culture with coloured pottery and the beginning of that Chinese farming culture which had such incredible continuity. (Yang-shao is an archaeological site in the Honan highlands, near the Hwang Ho.) The east Asian culture shares with the other early great cultures, the river civilizations, the stimulus of an accentuated pulsation of nature, of a life-dispensing water rhythm. It differs from them all in its duration. It was never conclusively overrun by nomadic tribes, by peoples on horseback; and its farmer's awareness of earth and sky, with the feeling of its own permanence, must have become stronger and stronger, perhaps finally leading to the foundation of ancestor-worship in Confucianism and the desire for male descendants. The rhythmic course of nature is incessant and the resurrection of these farmers from every catastrophe indefatigable.

Catastrophes continually occurred. The monsoon rains begin to die away over the loess highlands, towards the dry area of Inner Asia. About 19 in. fall in Shansi, but the variation in annual rainfall is between 27.5 and 7.8 in. The monsoon movement may be diverted cyclonically or by the trellis-work of the landscape's relief. In spite of the capillary rise of water in the soil, regional droughts and dry periods are the rule in a district which is short of water in any case. In A.D. 298, 300,000 people, driven by a great drought, emigrated southwards from Kansu, Shansi and Shensi to Szechwan and Honan. The Yangtze lowlands partly owe their increase in population to droughts in the north. But this northern region remained the great source of population and civilization.

So it is understandable that here, in the land bordering the dry country, irrigation and other stimuli from the Middle East were imported at an early date, probably via the celebrated "Oasis route". In the third millennium an Inner Asian chain of oases had already become a transcontinental route (Kolb).

But cultural influences also emanated from south and south-east Asia. And thus we find a highly developed way of life as early as the Shang period (1450—1050 B.C.). It was a farming culture with fortified towns on the edge of the highlands, facing the great lowlands, with metal money and trade, with handicrafts and bronze weapons. The pottery was supplemented by bronze vessels. The irrigation system rose up the mountain slopes from the valleys in regular terraces. Communal work on the building of canals and the control of water made writing, a counting system and state organization necessary. The great culture was there. Wheat and rice were added to the previous crop of millet (kaoliang). Cattle and horses from the interior of the continent were domesticated. Irrigation and planting rhythms demanded an understanding of the year's cycle. So this civilization began the science of measuring the stars. Astronomers were busy at court. Two of these imperial astronomers who overlooked the calculation of an eclipse of the sun (which was obviously already possible) paid for their scientific negligence with their lives. The event is handed down in the oldest Chinese book of records, the Shou-Ching. It is the oldest eclipse of the sun about which we have information. By calculating backwards with the help of the cycle of eclipses, it must have taken place on October 13, 2128 B.C. (Mädler).

Recently astronomical research was faced with the question whether the rapidly expanding Crab Nebula, in the constellation Taurus, could have begun its expansion approximately 900 years ago as an exploding star, a so-called nova. In fact, a new, exceptionally bright star in the place of the present-day Crab Nebula was actually described in Chinese annals for the year 1054. This confirmed not only a suspicion, but a theory. Great reliability must be attributed to Chinese documentary information until far into the first millennium B.C., since it is often verifiable from statements about eclipses.

The Shou-Ching, already mentioned, gives the view of life prevalent in the Chinese early period. Clothed in myth, the story is of rivers running wild in north China and even of the first taming of the Hwang Ho. Both daemonic and beneficent powers control the dramatic and the quietly unfolding process in the landscape. Man, with his individuality and thoughts, is woven into this process. His intimate link with the soil is transmitted to his art. "Landscape is the central theme of Chinese painting", and in it, too, we encounter the "interpenetration of spirituality and feeling for nature" (Emil Preetorius).

Chinese man has created his peculiarly autochthonous cultural edifice, in obedience to the elementary cycle and throughout the constant stream of generations and changing currents of the spirit. Modern China, too, after an overhasty leap into the industrial world revolution of the present, has again given the fostering of nature first place, and has placed industry "in the service of agriculture". Its latest technical works of river control, damming, irrigation and its vast plan to lead the high-water masses of the Yangtzekiang to the Hwang Ho, are in keeping with the gigantic proportions of the continent and its rivers, and worthy of the audacious achievements of its ancestors, the Great Wall and the Imperial Canal. The law of the landscape runs through the space and time of the Chinese world.

# China: A Story in Photographs     *by Emil Schulthess*

My efforts to compile a book describing modern China in photographs go back a long way. Several years ago I sent full details of the journey I had planned to the then Swiss Ambassador so that he would have a clear picture of what I wanted to do. I was also in touch with the Embassy of the Chinese People's Republic in Berne. However, my travel proposals were too comprehensive and led into very remote regions, so that in spite of repeated efforts the project came to nothing and I postponed my Chinese venture for the time being.

A few years later Dr. Hans Keller got in touch with me. He was on the point of leaving to take up his new post as Swiss Ambassador in Peking. He told me that he had followed my work for years, knew all my publications, and would like to offre his help if I was still interested in doing a book about China. I explained my former fruitless efforts to him and gave him photostats of the relevant correspondence with new, modified travel plans as well as some of my earlier books which might be helpful during his coming discussions in Peking.

A year went by before the first positive sign came from Peking. In the early summer of 1964 I was informed by the Chinese Embassy in Berne that my visa was ready. It took some time to explain to the Chinese diplomats in Berne that, as a first step, questions about weather conditions in specific regions at different seasons would have to be cleared up, that it was important to coordinate the stages of my journey with the dates of special events inside China, and above all that a minimum of time was necessary for careful preparation. At last it was agreed that it would be preferable to begin my journey in the autumn.

Although I had submitted four different travel programmes to Peking the year before, not a single one of my proposals was formally approved by either the Chinese Embassy in Berne or the authorities in Peking. All these details, so they told me in Berne, would be settled verbally with the Information Service of the Ministry for Foreign Affairs in Peking.

At the beginning of September 1964 I took off from Zurich-Kloten airport with a substantial load of photographic equipment, arriving in Peking the next afternoon via Prague, Moscow, Omsk and Irkutsk. During the first week I had discussion after discussion with the appropriate authorities. It took a lot of stubbornness, perseverance and truly Chinese patience to convince the right quarters that taking the photographs for a large volume of pictures made special demands. Supported by officials of the Swiss Embassy, I fought for permission to visit certain regions that were of exceptional importance for the contents, structure and documentary value of the book I planned. Only after a conversation with Mrs. Kung Peng, the Assistant Minister for Foreign Affairs in Peking, who showed great interest in the idea of a photographic book about China, was I given special permission to travel through the Yangtzekiang gorges and to the district of Kweilin—areas that had previously been closed to western correspondents for years.

Six months after returning from the first journey I decided to make a second trip. I was driven to this decision not only because of the bad weather conditions that had made it impossible for me to take a number of photographs I thought important, but even more because I did not think that I could do justice to a pictorial account of China after a single stay in the country. The further connexions and contacts of this second visit created new possibilities for photographic observation and analytical understanding which fulfilled my expectations.

The routes of my various trips inside China are marked on the sketch-map opposite. Including the flights to and from Zurich, I covered about 25,000 miles by air, some 2,500 of them on internal Chinese routes, and another 9,500 miles by rail, which involved 300 hours' travel on the Chinese railways. I covered the stretch of 700 miles between Chunking and Wuhan by river steamer and I used cars as additional means of transport in and around the towns I visited.

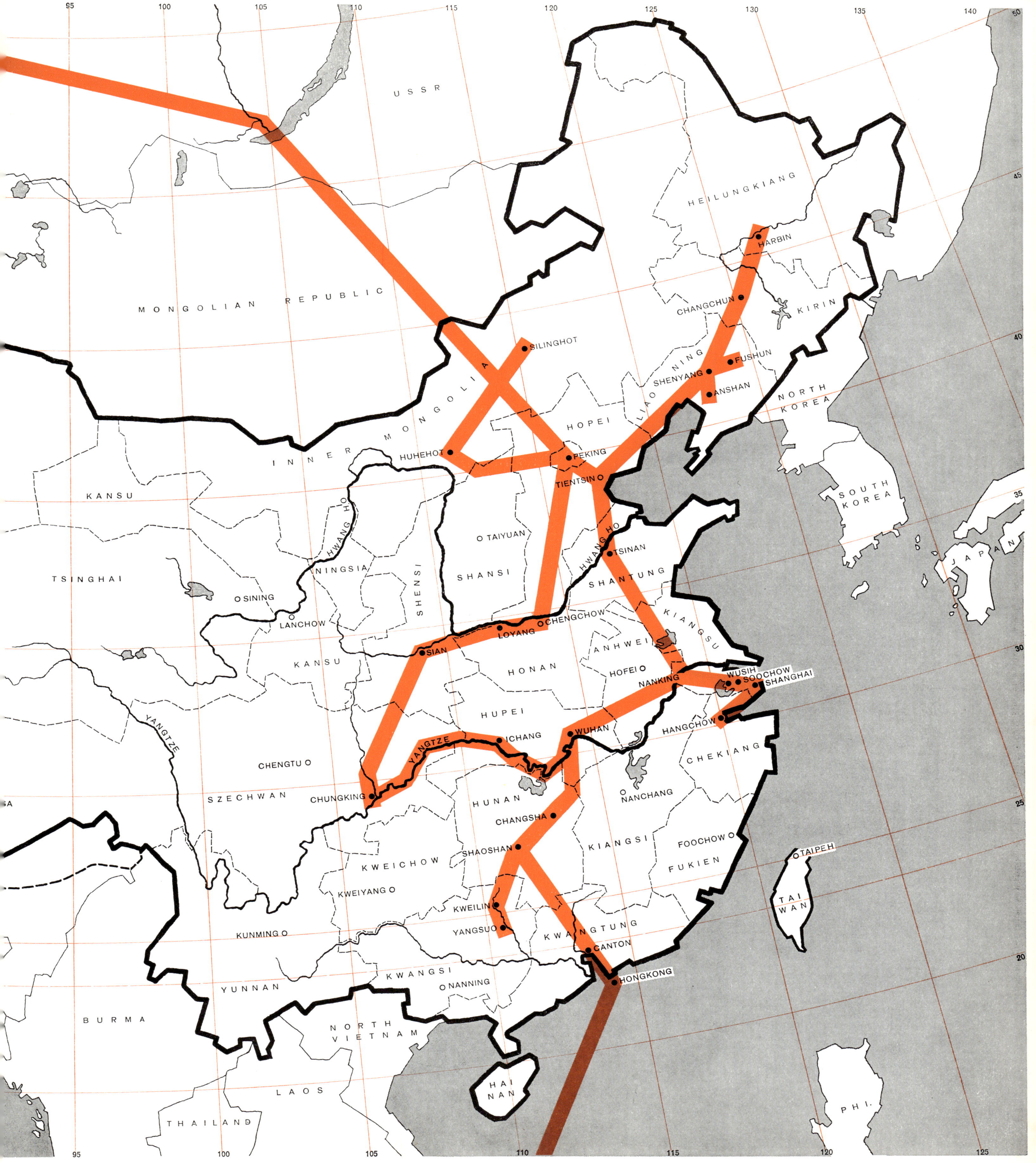

USSR

HEILUNGKIANG

MONGOLIAN REPUBLIC

HARBIN

CHANGCHUN

KIRIN

SILINGHOT

LIAONING

FUSHUN

SHENYANG

ANSHAN

NORTH KOREA

INNER MONGOLIA

HOPEI

KANSU

HUHEHOT

PEKING

TIENTSIN

SOUTH KOREA

HWANG HO

TAIYUAN

TSINAN

JAPAN

NINGSIA

SHANSI

HWANG HO

SHANTUNG

TSINGHAI

SINING

LANCHOW

SHENSI

CHENGCHOW

KIANGSU

LOYANG

ANHWEI

KANSU

HONAN

HOFEI

WUSIH SOOCHOW

SIAN

NANKING

SHANGHAI

HUPEI

HANGCHOW

CHENGTU

ICHANG

WUHAN

CHEKIANG

YANGTZE

YANGTZE

SZECHWAN

CHUNGKING

HUNAN

NANCHANG

CHANGSHA

KIANGSI

KWEICHOW

SHAOSHAN

FOOCHOW

FUKIEN

KWEIYANG

TAIPEH

KWEILIN

TAI WAN

YANGSUO

KWANGTUNG

KUNMING

CANTON

HONGKONG

YUNNAN

KWANGSI

NANNING

BURMA

NORTH VIETNAM

HAI NAN

PHI.

LAOS

THAILAND

# Wusih / Tai-hu

無錫

Following useful discussions in the Information Department of the Foreign Ministry in Peking, we fixed my first journey to Southwest China. Before a journey can begin, one must still have the appropriate written travel permit showing the destinations and the probable length of stay in each place. The document is procured by the officials of the "Travel Service", who are of great assistance to the traveller in China and who also provide interpreters. During my first week in Peking I was accompanied by a German-speaking interpreter, who astonished me during our tour of the Revolutionary Museum by his fluent commentary and his polished diction. However, when we went to the Peking Zoo, I was surprised to find that he did not know the names of common animals, nor could he translate my questions to the zoo staff. Since there are many more English-speaking interpreters available, I changed my interpreter and found in Mr. Lin Yen-chieh a likable young man who did his job very satisfactorily. There are advantages in keeping the same interpreter, and Mr. Lin went with me on practically all my travels.

After travelling for hours in a Chinese train on the Peking–Shanghai route, through the low-lying plains of the Lower Yangtze Basin, we arrived at the rail ferry shortly before Nanking. The train was split into three sections, and as we were in the middle section, our coach was put on to the centre track. The manœuvering and the crossing of the Yangtzekiang took nearly two hours. We preferred to leave our stay in Nanking until the return journey, so we carried on to Wusih, where we were met by Mr. Chin Hsun, who had been notified of our arrival by a wire from the "Travel Service Peking". Using a Polish-made limousine, we drove through the city to our hotel, which stood on an eminence overlooking the celebrated Tai-hu Lake. I immediately asked for a conference with Mr. Chin about the programme for the next few days. It was at this point that I discovered that I must have left my ball point pen in the compartment in the train.

Mr. Chin was certain it would be found; and even as we were talking there came a telephone message from the station to say the pen was already on its way to the hotel.

By displaying some samples of my work that I always carry with me on my travels I managed to convince Mr. Chin that my needs and intentions were rather different from those of the normal tourist. I explained that I was an early riser and did not leave it until after breakfast to begin my work, but started before the sun came up.

Next morning, as arranged, the car was waiting at 5 a.m. We drove to the Li Gardens, a large park with romantic nooks, bridges, pavilions and ponds. But the gates were still locked: they were not opened until 6 a.m. It took Mr. Chin a long time to rouse a park-keeper out of his slumber—and so we missed the sunrise.

1 *Pagoda in the Li Garden on the bank of the Li-hu near Wusih, Kiangsu Province.*

"Reveille" the following morning was at 4 a.m. I had found on the map a spot on the Li-hu from which I could photograph the sunrise on the surface of the water, and we drove off in the direction of the lake while it was still dark, but found the way blocked at one point by road repairs. We had to turn back and make a time-wasting diversion. Dawn began to break, showing promise of a wonderful day. We came to a bridge that divided the small Li-hu from the great Tai-hu and had to be crossed if we were to reach the spot I had worked out to be especially favourable for seeing the sunrise. But Mr. Chin pointed out that we were not allowed to cross the bridge; the terrain on the other side was outside the area covered by my permit. My nervousness grew with the increasing brightness of the eastern horizon. After I had promised to assume full responsibility for any complications that might ensue, we raced over the bridge to the spot I had chosen. Working in feverish haste, I just managed to get my tripod and camera set up before the pale red of the sun's disc rose above the misty horizon.

2 *Sunrise over the Li-hu near Wusih.* Indescribable peace and stillness lie over the lake. The sun's growing intensity bathes the scene in fiery colour. In the early dawn a few boats are already gliding over the water—Wusih fishermen looking for mussels and crabs.

After breakfast we drove to a jetty. At my request Mr. Chin organized a motor boat to take us to a small lake near the Tai-hu. Fishing was forbidden in the Tai-hu at the moment—it was still the close season.

9

8

3 *Catching fish in the small lake near the Tai-hu, Wusih.* In the shallow water long bamboo strips are driven into the bed of the lake to form large enclosures. These are left open at one point to allow the fish to reach the inside. At various points the stakes form small traps, from which the fish, swimming along the wall of stakes, cannot escape. The fishermen row to these spots and catch the trapped fish in nets attached to long bamboo poles.

4 *Fishing net near Wusih.* The wide plain around Wusih is intersected by innumerable canals. Here and there, fishing nets stand out above the horizon, hung up to dry on tall bamboo poles.

5 *Ship-yard, the Tung-kang Commune near Wusih.* The Tung-kang Commune near Wusih adjoined a small ship-yard in which several boats were being made. The work was fascinating to watch. There are very few mechanical tools; everything is still done by hand. Even the boring of the large holes in the planking is done without mechanical aid. The man lines up the drill, around which a cord is wound, at the desired spot and the girl rotates the drill by energetically pulling the cord to and fro. Using this method, it is surprising how quickly the work gets done.

The Tung-kang Commune lies outside Wusih, to the south. The fertile land is intensively cultivated and every available foot is tilled. The broad landscape is resplendent with a variety of colours ranging from the succulent yellow of the fields of rape to the tender green of young rice.

The director of the Tung-kang Commune took us into the administration building. The architecture of the house and the splendour of the interior revealed that we were in the home of one of the former great land owners. The Commune was founded in 1958, when the whole of China was divided up into 24,000 People's Communes. (Today, as a result of the bitter experience of the "Great Leap Forward", the total number of Communes arising from a redistribution on the basis of economic rationalization has grown to 72,000.) The population of the commune is about 15,000, of whom approximately one-fifth work in the town. The commune is divided into 13 Brigades, and these again are split up into 137 production groups. The production figures

are said to have gone up by 25 % since 1958. Power stations have been constructed, so that today most of the irrigation installations can be driven by electricity.

6 *Rice planting in the Tung-kang Commune.* Spring cultivation is in full swing. Planks of wood are pushed to and fro over the rice beds, which are slippery and covered with manure water, until they are absolutely flat. This strenuous work is mostly carried out by the younger generation.

7 *A Rice-sower of the Tung-kang Commune.* The sowers are given the precious seed carefully weighed out in baskets and scatter the rice grains as evenly as possible over the rice beds. This work is for experienced hands only and is therefore usually entrusted to the older workers. After this the beds are carefully covered with ashes. When the rice shoots reach a certain height and carry their tender green buds they are scrupulously cleared of every single weed-shoot—a most tedious job.

8 *Peasant girl from the outskirts of Wusih at her midday meal.* On the way back to the town we pass a settlement. The families are sitting at their midday meal before their houses. The staple food is of course rice and fish—this fertile region has for centuries been called "the land of fish and rice".

9 *Worker in the silk-spinning mill No.1, Wusih.* The girl empties one measure of white silk cocoons after another into the soaking bath. This permits a gradual softening of the hard cocoons, which have been graded for size and are measured out as required. Subsequently the silk thread, which is about 1,000 yards long on an average, is wound from the cocoons on to a reel.

Silk is a Chinese discovery. The origin of its use for adornment and decoration is said to lie in the Chinese age of the "mythical rulers". Legend relates how in 2640 B.C. the Empress Hsi Ling-shih discovered silk, personally cared for the silkworms, encouraged the planting of mulberry trees and even invented a loom.
The Chinese managed to keep the secret of silk-making to themselves, just as they preserved the secrets of porcelain-making. When, after 3,000 years of

monopoly, the first silkworm eggs were smuggled over the Chinese frontier to Korea and later from there to Japan, India and finally to Constantinople, Chinese brocade weaving, during the Han and Tang Dynasties (206 B.C. to A.D. 906) was already in full bloom. Silk was worth its weight in gold. It is said to have been an aristocratic privilege to possess it and even to practise the art of silk cultivation.

Geographically, the main silk production centres of white or cultivated silk are found in the southern half of the continent and of wild or tussore silk in the northern half. China's share of the world's total production of wild silk is roughly 80—90%. Her share of the world's cultivated silk, about 30—40%, may appear less important; but it takes pride of place at least as far as Europe is concerned because considerable quantities of tussore do reach Western markets, whereas Japan, who is the world's biggest producer of cultivated silk, is also its greatest consumer.

The gleaming white Wusih silk, the matchless tussores, hand woven from handwound thread, such as Shantung and Honan pongee from the provinces of those names, are particularly prized in the markets of the world.

From the Hsi-shan mountain one gets an extensive panoramic view over the town of Wusih, with its many smoking chimney-stacks. The region's present-day light and heavy industries have developed to a point where they are not far behind those of Nanking. A large power station, built between Wusih and Soochow in 1958, provides power for the 600,000 inhabitants.

10  *Waterway in the Interior of Wusih.* A feature of Wusih is the extensive network of canals, used even today for the transport of a good proportion of the city's freight. The arched bridges and the picturesque corners, with houses standing directly on the water's edge, are typical of most of the towns in the canal system of the Lower Yangtze Basin. In contrast to the settlements in the north, the roads of this area are not laid out rigidly north-south and east-west. In place of wide roads there are canals, for which there would be no room in the densely inhabited settlements.

Recently, in order to allow more space for the increasing road traffic, one or two canals have been filled in. New housing estates and industrial complexes are sited outside the city centre, which thus retains its traditional appearance.

11  *The Great Canal (Imperial Canal) inside Wusih.* The waterway seems hopelessly blocked by an indescribably confused mass of boats. Yet if one observes the fascinating bustle for a while, it becomes apparent that a certain order is maintained even in this apparent chaos, that a lane opens up as if accidentally, and long convoys pass easily through on their way up-river or down-river.

The first stage in the building of the Imperial Canal, begun twenty-five centuries ago in several different sections and at different times, was intended to connect up the southern lakeland area and the extremity of the Yangtze delta for a length of some 200 miles. At the beginning of the 7th century, at the time of the Sui Dynasty, the waterway was extended, in the north to beyond the one-time capital, Loyang, and in the south up to Hangchow. Such a waterway running north and south would have been particularly important because most of the rivers between the northern and southern regions run from west to east.

For the ruling classes in the states to the north, silk and brocade were attractive commodities that could be brought to them by canal. The extension to the canal also made it possible to procure large quantities of food from the more favoured rice-growing provinces of the Yangtze Basin. Thus the grain transport in one year during the Sui Dynasty (A.D. 960—1279) exceeded 600,000 tons. During the period of Mongol rule at the end of the 13th century, the Imperial Canal was extended to Peking, and two centuries later the northern part was widened and improved under the Ming Dynasty. The Grand Canal, which today connects Peking and Hangchow, traverses the four provinces of Hopei, Shantung, Kiangsu and Chekiang, runs through a number of important towns such as Ningpo, Shaohing, Kashing, Soochow, Wutsin and Chinkiang, and forms a connecting link with the great river system of the Yangtzekiang, the Hwai Ho and the Hwang Ho. Its total length of over 1,000 miles makes it the largest internal waterway in the world.

Work has been in progress for some years now to deepen, widen and extend this great canal with the aim of making it navigable by motor ships up to 2,000 G.R.T. But the canal system does not only serve shipping. It is equally useful for the drainage, irrigation, flood control, water supply and power supply of the Lower Yangtze Basin, which, with its population of over 100 millions, is part of the key economic and cultural area of China.

In the market place in Wusih there is a colourful scene of bustle and activity. An unimaginable variety of merchandise from food to textiles, pottery and household goods are offered for sale. There is time to bargain, compare, examine and gossip. Thick smoke, clouds of hot steam and exotic odours surround the food stalls, where the owners prepare all kinds of appetizing dishes.

We paid a visit to the Hui-shan factory in Wusih, where pottery figurines are made. The statuettes are made by the thousand and painted in vivid colours in a number of workshops. Apart from a small number of models representing historical figures, the main production is of figures from the modern age. Whole armies of clay soldiers in heroic postures were lined up on the tables, along with hundreds of peasant men and women, getting the finishing touch before being carefully packed for despatch. Several men were gathered around one table — these were the designers of the statuettes, discussing a new design. On asking which kind of figure sold best, historical or modern, I was told that the demand for present-day personalities was so great it could hardly be met. The one in greatest demand was the bust of Mao Tse-tung, made in various shapes and sizes. One had to admire the dexterity of the workers, but there could be no two opinions about the taste displayed in these figures, which accord with "the requirements of the people".

On the evening of our final day in the neighbourhood of Wusih we went to the Turtle's Head Islet and climbed the small hill that stands at the north-east corner of the 770 square miles of the Tai-hu. My companions, Mr. Chin and Mr. Lin, were in the best of spirits. I told them I was satisfied with the result of my stay and that I was grateful to them for the way they had helped me. I advised them to hurry, for we had hundreds of steps before us and were anxious to reach the top before the sun went down.

12 *Sunset over the Western Hills on the Tai-hu*. My hopes of getting an uninterrupted view across the wide expanse of water were dashed. The top of the hill, on which stood a small pavilion resting on bright-red pillars, was thickly covered with Scotch pines, but I forced my way through the branches just the same. The glorious sunset made its impression on my companions, too. They softly began to sing a melody together.

# Soochow

蘇 州

A train journey southward of under an hour brought us to Soochow. The foreigner who applies in Peking for permission to visit Soochow will not be refused; indeed he will be encouraged to visit what was the capital during the Wu Kingdom, some 1,000 years ago. The town is also a favourite holiday place for Chinese, and all the year round Chinese holiday-makers come to see the celebrated gardens with their splendid temples, pavilions and pagodas of the Sung, Yuan, Ming and Ching Dynasties. Chinese visitors show considerable interest in the products of ancient Chinese culture. For their part, the government are doing their best to make Soochow into a complete shop window, to prove to the foreigner their efforts to preserve places of historical importance.

It rained without ceasing during our stay. The Chinese we met did not seem unduly depressed about the rain, although they were obviously sorry not to have better weather in which to display the treasures of the place people were already calling "Heaven on Earth" centuries ago.

On our first evening there was a harvest festival, the Festival of the Autumn Moon, and we were invited to it. But by the evening the weather left no doubt that the annual occasion would be a wash-out and that the full moon would be concealed behind the swollen rain clouds. There were great crowds in front of the gate, the entrance to the "Wang-shih-yuan". Our escorts managed to get us through the tightly pressed crowds of sightseers, and we saw that rows of people were sitting packed together in the temples, on galleries and in the pavilions around the pond, around the stone statuary groups in the cliff-gardens and on the bridges of the gardens. Many of them, mostly the young ones, were singing in chorus, while others argued or gossiped. The whole scene was a pleasing contrast to the usual monotonous grey of every day. I had my electronic flash outfit with me, but I could not bring myself to disturb this fascinating scene, with its shadow and half shadows, by using it. The rain had ceased and the moon—although probably little noticed by many of those present—came out for a moment or two.

13   *Canal in the centre of Soochow, Kiangsu Province*. For the European, the picturesque arched bridges that span the canals almost automatically bring Venice to mind. There are a number of resemblances, it is true, but there are also great differences. For all its beauty and uniqueness, Venice has the character of a museum. Soochow, on the other hand, is hard, living reality that retains its splendour by reason of a number of romantic attributes. Everywhere in the winding alleys of crowded houses there are multitudes of children, who surround the stranger and refuse to leave him. If he wants to take a photograph of them, some of them will take to flight and hide around the next corner, while others, less shy, will take up a grotesque attitude of military "attention" and thus make it impossible to get any kind of natural picture.

14   *A young artist in the Cho-cheng-yuan Garden in Soochow*. The 18-year-old art student Chen Hui-chin was sitting in a corner of the garden concentrating on her drawing-board. She was drawing a rose and did not allow herself to be put off for a second by the questions I put to her through the interpreter. When she had finished her training, she told us, she wanted to be a pattern designer in the Soochow Arts and Crafts Factory.

15   *In the Embroidery Institute, Soochow*. Among the most popular embroidery designs are floral motifs with red roses. The embroidered products this Institute turns out in great numbers are mainly intended for export or for presentation to statesmen from friendly countries or other high dignitaries visiting China. In one room four girls were putting the final touches to a large portrait of President Nasser, made from photographs. The Western visitor is not likely to be greatly impressed by the artistic value of such products, but he cannot help but admire the zeal and concentration of the embroiderers.

The map had shown me that there was a mountain in the vicinity of Soochow called Lin-yen-shan, from the top of which I thought I would be able to get a better view of the surrounding terrain. The hilly rises inside Soochow, being covered with dense trees, do not afford any spectacular views of the outlying plains. Our journey to Lin-yen-shan began with a run through the suburbs, past newly-built factories and housing estates, evidence of increasing industrialization.

After some 15 miles we reached the foot of the mountain, where parked buses and lorries showed that the mountain must be a favourite resort of the Chi-

nese on their outings. The car was parked near the refreshment kiosk, the only saloon among the many vehicles, and we prepared to climb the mountain on foot.

After about half an hour, climbing through a wonderful pine forest on a steep paved path, we reached the 650 ft level, to find that temple buildings took up the whole of the thickly-wooded ridge higher up. Countless schoolchildren, students and workers were crowding into the gardens and the interior of the temple. I bought a picture postcard in the temple yard and saw from it that the peak of the mountain must lie behind the high walls surrounding the temple area. I told Mr. Pan that the view must be better from there and that I should like to get up to this point to take some pictures. However the gate, the only public entrance, was unfortunately locked. But I was not satisfied, and said with a show of annoyance that there must be another entrance, and began to descend to search for a way in below the temple area. We clambered up and down along the steep slopes below the temple wall and finally reached the summit, where we found groups of schoolchildren resting, Pioneers wearing red neckerchieves. The visibility was unfortunately not very clear and I used a red filter to cut down the effect of the haze. The Pioneers followed my activities with great interest. Whenever I moved close to a group of them, they would begin to applaud loudly. One group was about to descend, but before they took their departure they once again enthusiastically applauded the visitor!

16  *Fields at the foot of Mount Lin-yen-shan, near Soochow.* Between the canals lie fields of rice, millet, soya beans, peanuts, sesame, rape and cotton. Here and there isolated farm buildings stand at the canal's edge. The low-lying floodable areas are mainly sown with rice in summer and wheat in winter. The land higher up bears maize, sweet potatoes or runner beans, and there are also orchards.

Two harvests a year are common in the Yangtze Basin, thanks to the mild winter climate. In good years record harvests are quite common. For this reason the plains are one of the areas which produce a surplus of food. The extra crops are sent to central distribution depots lying on important canals. The Yangtze Basin is covered with a network of canals of all sizes, forming the greatest concentration of artificial waterways in China—according to official figures, their total length is more than 62,000 miles.

It worried our guide that I was more interested in the little everyday events of life on the canals than in the tourist attractions. If my time had not been so limited, I would have been most interested to sail in a junk down the Imperial Canal to Hangchow, our next stop.

17  *Towing boats along the Grand Canal near Soochow.* We saw them from a long way off, towing their boat at the end of a long rope. We stood on the Pao-tai Bridge and waited for some time for the slowly-moving women to reach us. The wind was against them, and the mother and her two daughters had to exert all their strength. The sight of the hard-working women and girls was something one could not forget, as one wondered where they came from and where they were bound for.

# Hangchow

杭 州

Hangchow, the capital of Chekiang Province, lies on the bay of the same name at the mouth of the Yangtzekiang. Here ends the Grand Canal at its southern-most point. The medieval chroniclers and adventurers praised Hangchow, the imperial city of the Sung Dynasty, more highly even than the glory and splendour of Venice. "The greatest city in the world" wrote Marco Polo and Brother Oderic, "with palaces, gardens and mausoleums of art-loving emperors, a city of lagoons with 12,000 bridges, 3,000 public baths fed by warm springs, with streets brimming with turbulent life, as smooth as the floor of a ballroom and so wide that they could take nine coaches side by side".

The tide of a cruel history destroyed the erstwhile greatness of Hangchow. It began with the onslaught of the Mongols in the 13th Century, that reduced the libraries, the walls and the monuments to rubble and ashes, and ended with the destruction wreaked by the Taiping Rebels, the Chinese Anabaptists. In the spring of 1862 hordes of them took the town, burnt it completely to the ground and murdered 600,000 people. The remainder of the population perished from starvation and disease, and those who still survived, a contemporary chronicler tells us, drowned themselves in the canals, which were soon choked with corpses, or in the West Lake, so that "a man could walk half a *li* (250 yards) across the bodies as if he were on a footpath".

Hangchow never recovered from this dreadful atrocity. The West Lake remains, embedded in wooded hills, on which are scattered the evidence of the former size and splendour of Hangchow, the "Heavenly City of the Chinese Graces".

The Hangchow Hotel in which we stayed lies in the immediate vicinity of the celebrated West Lake. We met groups of tourists from East Germany, Czechoslovakia, England and New Zealand. Also enjoying the serenity of this scenic paradise were visitors from Africa and tourists from neighbouring Asiatic countries. In the great dining room there was a babel of different languages. Here I was made to realize for the first time the difficulties the "Travel Service" must have in mobilizing a sufficiently large army of interpreters.

On the first day Mr. Yuan, our guide in Hangchow, insisted that we see a sanatorium and other modern attractions.

18 *View of the Western Hills from the Railway Workers Trade Union Sanatorium, Chekiang*. The sanatorium was built outside the town because of the bracing air due to the many trees covering the hilly landscape. The sanatorium not only takes in convalescents but it can also be used by "model workers" who distinguish themselves by outstanding performance. As a rule the Chinese guests spend one or two weeks' convalescence here.

Ever since we left the hotel in the early morning, Mr. Yuan had carried with him a small plastic bag, and I became more and more curious about its contents as the day wore on. Just before noon we crossed the famous "Soo Causeway" to reach the Hua-chiang goldfish pond—and the secret was revealed. Mr. Yuan took breadcrumbs from his plastic bag and began to feed the goldfish.

The weather showed signs of improvement. That evening I arranged with Mr. Yuan and the driver to travel next morning before daybreak, in order not to miss the sunrise over the West Lake. The clear night and the stars in the night sky showed why I thought it worthwhile to leave at 4 a.m. The alarm clock, that I had put under my pillow so as not to wake the other guests, went off. I looked out of the window and saw some stars—so it looked as if the weather would be good.

Rising at 4 a.m., we drove to the lake, left the car and hauled the bulky equipment to the quayside, finally putting it down at the Ping-hu-chiu-yueh, the "Pavilion of the Calm Lake and Autumn Moon". A few fishermen gazed at me in amazement as I set up tripods and cameras on a projecting terrace.

19 *The West Lake after sunrise, Hangchow*. An indescribably beautiful morning. The wind dropped for a short while, leaving the surface of the water like an enchanting mirror. I was trying to include in the picture the drooping willow branches that reminded me of a brush-written Chinese character and by a wonderful chance a fisherman in his boat glided by just at the right moment.

On our way back to the hotel we had to pass a point-duty policeman, already at his post despite the fact that at this ungodly hour there was no traffic to be seen on the roads. Seeing us coming, the policeman immediately switched the traffic lights from red to green.

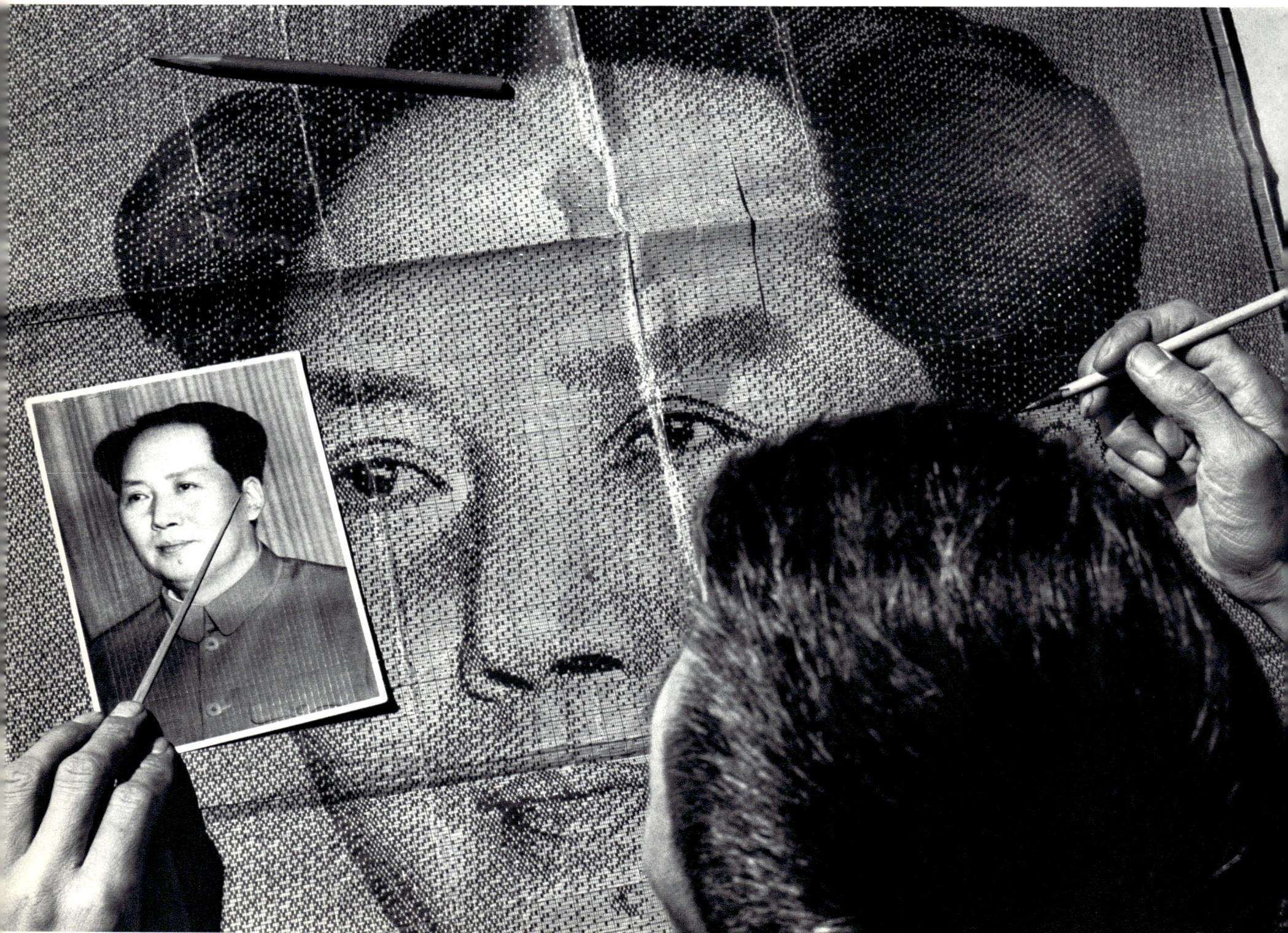

22

23

West of Hangchow, near the Lung-chin Dragon Spring, there are extensive tea plantations on the slopes and in the valleys of the green-covered mountain ranges that form part of the South Chinese mountain country. This is where the "Lung-chin" green tea, famed both at home and abroad, is cultivated. The fertile soil, the mild climate and the plentiful rain all the year round provide the right conditions for the outstanding quality of the tea.

20  *Tea-pickers of the "Mei-ya-wu" Brigade, Hangchow.* The "Mei-ya-wu" Brigade, part of the West Lake Commune of Hangchow, numbers some 1,000 people, who look after an area of 770 *mo*, just under 2,000 acres. The young director of the Brigade told me that "before the liberation" the yield was only 65 to 70 lb of dried tea per *mo* but that by 1957 it had risen to 180 lb per *mo*.

21  *Drying tea at the tea-processing plant of the "Mei-ya-wu" Brigade, Hangchow.*
The fires in the ovens are kept as far as possible at a constant level by continuously feeding in dried twigs. The green leaves are dried in troughs built into the ovens. Squatting in front of the troughs, men and women keep the leaves on the move and see to it that their contents reach the right stage of dryness. The group in the picture with a red pennant hanging over them are the most successful at the moment, but the flag will change to another group as soon as they do better than this one.

The "Chien-tsao" Commune, where we made a brief stop to see the seasonal workers in the field, has a small hospital attached to it. The foreign visitor is warmly invited to see the amenities such as school buildings, club rooms and hospitals. Here and elsewhere on our travels, the picture was very much the same. The amenities, especially the hospitals and clinics, are spruced up for the visitor from abroad. Despite this, the tourist from the West finds conditions crude and primitive. To be fair, however, one must remember that only a little time ago few would have dreamed of such medical and social facilities in the country districts of China.

22  *The forecourt of an agricultural machinery repair shop in the "Chien-tsao" Commune, Hangchow.* To mark the coming National Day, 1st October, banners are hung out, displaying the three most important slogans we saw all over China: "Long live the General Line of the Party", "Long live the Great Leap Forward" and "Long live the People's Commune".

Hangchow has been connected with the silk industry for centuries. Its brocades became famous all over the world, and even today the Hangchow silk experts manage to produce an astonishing variety of designs.
The silk-spinning mill we visited was the Tu-ching-hsün, which, with 1,700 workers and 300 machines, had produced $2^1/_2$ million yards of silk materials in the previous year.

23  *Designer in the Tu-ching-hsün silk spinning mill, Hangchow.* Since 1949 this mill has been producing, in addition to the traditional products, great numbers of "portraits in silk" of Chinese leaders. As the picture shows, these are prepared for mass production from photographs. The best selling silk portrait is that of Mao Tse-tung; yet it is not only the Chinese leaders whose portraits are produced but also those of Marx, Engels, Lenin and others. One machine has for some time been fully employed in producing enormous quantities of portraits of Stalin.

# Shanghai

上 海

"Gone the glitter and glamour; gone the pompous wealth beside naked starvation; gone the strange excitement of a polyglot and many-sided city; gone the island of western civilization in the vast slum that was Shanghai.

"Goodbye to all that: the well-dressed Chinese in their chauffeured cars behind bullet-proof glass, the gangsters, the shakedowns, the kidnappers; the exclusive foreign clubs. Goodbye to all the night life: the gilded singing girl in her enamelled hairdo, the tight-fitting gown with the slit skirt breaking at the silk-clad hip; the hundred dance halls and the thousands of taxi dolls; the opium dens and the gambling halls; the sailors in their smelly bars and friendly brothels on Szechwan Road, the myriad short-time whores and pimps, busily darting in and out of the alleyways; the innumerable shops spilling with silks, jades, embroideries, porcelains and all the wares of the east; the beggars on every down town block and the scabby kids relieving themselves in the gutters while their mothers absently scratched for lice; the 'honey carts' hauling the nightsoil through the streets; the jungle free-for-all struggle for gold or survival and the daily tribute of unwanted babies and suicides floating in the canals; the armored white ships on the Wangpoo, 'protecting foreign lives and property'; gone the wickedest and most colourful city of the old Orient: Goodbye to all that."

Such were the words with which Edgar Snow, in his book *The Other Side of the River,* began the chapter on Shanghai, revisiting the city in 1960 for the first time after he had spent twelve years in China as the Asian correspondent of American newspapers before 1949—that is, before the Communist take-over.

24 *Long-range shot of part of the centre of Shanghai.*

Despite all the political upheavals, Shanghai has remained China's greatest port and the centre of her trade and industry; it has a population, including the inhabitants of the suburbs, of over ten millions. The city's distinguishing feature is the "Bund", the great promenade running along the Wangpoo River. The façades of the skyscrapers—the former business houses, hotels and banks run by European and Japanese managers who held the reins of the economy in their hands—give Shanghai, alone of all the cities of China, the appearance of a genuine metropolis.

25 *View over the Soochow River, Shanghai.* In the foreground, the Chapu Road Bridge; in the background the Szechwan Road Bridge, with the large Post Office building to its right. The densely populated quarters of the city, the crowded streets, the innumerable bicycles and pedicabs, the motor and trolley buses and the lorries packed with workers, are exactly the same as one sees in other towns and cities in China.

26 *Pedicab driver, Nanking Road, Shanghai.* The old-fashioned rickshaw is no longer allowed. The millions of rickshaw-pullers would have been thrown out of work if it had not been for the invention of the pedicab. Many of them are two-seaters and family-sized pedicabs are not uncommon.

27 *Morning exercises on the Bund.* Every morning, even before daybreak, groups of Chinese of all ages come to the Bund for gymnastic exercises. While other people hurry to their work, they exercise singly or in groups, young men and girls, men and women, and even older ones, who indulge in shadow-boxing. Opposite the Hopei Hotel, where we were living, spectators surrounded two fencers, who practise here every day.

Modern Shanghai is an important centre of Chinese industry. The products manufactured there range from antibiotics and disposable nappies to rolling mills and hydraulic presses, from television sets and cameras to motor car tyres and generators, from cars and ocean-going ships to sewing machines and fountain pens, from surgical instruments and X-ray apparatus to drills and diesel tractors.

28 *Hoardings in the grounds of "Food Factory No. 1", Shanghai.* Enormous placards with slogans intended to influence the political thinking of the working masses are to be seen not only in the streets and public squares but also in the grounds of the factories.

"Food Factory No. 1", taken over by the Communist government in 1949, today employs 3,000 workers, and produces over 300 products such as powdered milk, tomato puree, ice cream, sweets and a wide assortment of conserves. In the hot summer months the factory produces two million ice-cream sticks a day.

27X1管式大车胎

无接头内胎

中国橡胶工业公司上海分公司

9号 电话:374574总机

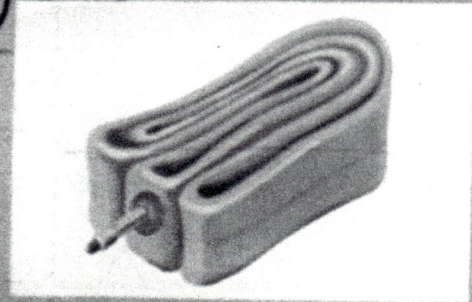

海
江南造船厂
1961年

## 32

Mr. Wang Heo-kang, our tireless guide in Shanghai, organised a visit to the "Heavy Industry Works", in which the first 12,000-ton hydraulic press had been erected. As this, the largest press ever built in China, was planned and built completely without foreign help, it is the pride and joy of the whole area.

29 *The 12,000-ton Hydraulic Press, Shanghai.* A 25-ton steel ingot is brought to the press under the supervision of the foreman, who gives his instructions to the cranedriver by hand-signals and by blowing a whistle. When the red-hot mass is in position, the engineer at the control console sets the machinery in motion by pressing the red button. The 70-foot high press, standing on a 300-ton base and four pillars each three feet in diameter, can forge ingots two to three hundred tons in weight, of the type used in heavy industry, in the manufacture of chemicals and the building of power stations.

At present there are said to be not more than two dozen hydraulic presses of this size in the world. Engineers and Chinese labourers built this one, despite the lack of skilled constructors and the dearth of the necessary technical know-how. Particularly difficult was the making of the four mighty pillars and the three cross-ties. Normally each pillar would be made out of a 100-ton steel ingot and forged with a 10,000-ton press, and the cross-ties would be built up out of various 100-ton steel forms. But no factory in China was capable of handling such enormous components at that time.

After much thought the construction engineers decided to make the pillars by welding together sections of cast steel and the cross-ties by building them up out of layers of steel plate.

Most difficult of all was the welding of the base-plate, the biggest and heaviest single part of the whole installation. To do this, 100 single steel sheets with a combined weight of 300 tons had to be put together. Another problem was lifting the base-plate to allow the welding to be done. The works had no crane capable of lifting 300-ton pieces. But the Chinese engineers and mechanics overcame even this problem with technical skill and using marvels of improvisation.

West of Shanghai lie acres of newly built industrial estates and the sprawling housing estates that surround them. These new estates, which have increased the area of Shanghai by a third, have been planned on the most modern lines and contain shopping centres, tall blocks of flats, hotels, schools, children's playgrounds, cinemas and theatres.

30 *View of the Wu-ching Chemical Factory, Shanghai.* The Wu-ching works started operating in October 1963, the chief product being artificial fertiliser. The machinery and installations were made by the Chinese themselves. Of the 2,800 workers, only 3 per cent had any experience when they started; the rest had previously been handcart men, rickshaw-pullers, barbers, etc.

31 *Evening on the International Harbour, Shanghai.* The docks on the west bank of the Wangpoo can handle six ships at a time. 50—60 ships a month tie up in Shanghai, discharging an average monthly total of 250,000 tons of cargo. The 2,600 dock workers are among the most highly paid in China, with an average wage of 85 yuan (about £12 or $36) a month. A small family will pay about 7 to 10 yuan a month for rent and spend 35 to 50 yuan on food. They will not spend much more than 20 yuan a year on clothing. They will be able to save a little towards buying a sewing machine, a radio set or a bicycle. But these things are very expensive. For a Chinese, buying a bicycle, for example, corresponds to the buying of a small car for a Western worker.

32 *Illuminations along the Bund skyline during the 1st May celebrations.* On the 1st May and 1st October holidays Shanghai is decorated overall. The main streets and the Bund are decked out with endless chains of electric light bulbs, lending an impressive appearance to the skyline. After dusk the people pour into the city centre to admire the illuminations.

From Shanghai we flew on to Nanking. We could hardly recognise Mr. Wang, who escorted us to the airport. Hitherto we had only seen him in his khaki working dress, but on this Sunday he surprised us by appearing in an elegant suit, with a white shirt and a well-knotted tie.

# Nanking

南 京

The Ilyushin 14 twin-engined plane taking us to Nanking made a wide circle over Shanghai's dense sea of houses and then set course westwards over the broad plains of Kiangsu Province. In the rays of the bright sunshine countless canals were reflected like lovely spiders' webs. I must confess that my fingers were itching to take a picture of these vast green lowlands, some of the most fertile in the world. But in order to avoid the temptation, I had my cameras put in with the rest of my baggage, since it is strictly forbidden to take photographs from the air. All my efforts to get special permission to do so had been in vain.

Chinese pilots take no risks. When the weather deteriorates the time table is not adhered to or flying may be simply stopped altogether.

The foreign passenger is given precedence in everything aboard the aircraft. He can select the best seat at the most suitable window and is the first to be served with refreshments. He is kept informed of the aircraft's position and about the rivers or mountain ranges the machine is passing over.

We flew along the eastern bank of the Tai-hu Lake and approached the hilly country south of Nanking. The aircraft made wide sweeping turns over the town, dropped down to cross the enormous span of the Yangtzekiang and landed punctually on the airfield at Nanking.

33 *Chung-shan Road, Nanking.* Nanking, the capital of Kiangsu Province, lies at the foot of a mountain range, whose spurs reach out to the south bank of the Yangtzekiang. The favourable position of the town for the crossing of the river, already known and used many centuries ago, makes Nanking an important link in the traffic from north to south. Here also the railway lines from Shanghai, Wushu and Tientsin all meet. A powerful train-ferry and ferry boats for other traffic connect the north and south banks of the river.

Nanking's position on these traffic routes and on China's greatest river has always been of strategic importance. The town, founded in the second century B.C. during the Han Period, has been the provisional seat of government from time to time during periods of crisis, the first time in the fourth to sixth century, then in the 12th century, in the Ming Period and finally in the Kuomintang era.

The selection of Nanking as the Kuomintang capital in April 1927 was a momentous political decision. At this time Chiang Kai-shek had to decide whether to follow the advice of the left wing who wanted to expropriate the great capitalists and the feudal lords, or whether to go along with the right wing, who supported collaboration with the great financiers and moderate land reform. In the event, he came down on the side of the latter. One result of this was that Shanghai, the wealthy city his troops were beleaguering, surrendered without a fight and the financial future of his government and fighting forces seemed assured. Similarly the great industrialists were relieved at the choice of Nanking as the capital, as the greater part of the still-young Chinese industry lay in the area of the Yangtzekiang: and the landowners were equally satisfied. The Yangtze plains had always been regarded as the most fertile agricultural area in China, and the great landowners thought they could see a better opening for the sale of their products if the capital were nearby. Thus Chiang Kai-shek's decision in the spring of 1927 was one of the reasons why nothing was done towards bringing about the urgently-needed social reform —and the Communists were able to make heavy political capital out of it.

During our stay in Nanking we were escorted by Mr. Chen Tao-yi of the "Travel Service" and Mr. Chang Shek-yu, a photographer and the Vice-President of the Nanking association of Chinese photographers. We drove to the harbour and went aboard a motor-boat that Mr. Chang had organised at my request for a trip on the Yangtzekiang.

34 *The Yangtzekiang near Nanking.* As we sailed upriver we saw several construction sites spanning the river, with nine massive pillars projecting from the water, the supports for the new Yangtze bridge. This second bridge will be much longer than the Wuhan bridge, the only other bridge spanning the Yangtze. Here in the lower reaches the river is much broader, and the wide approaches to the river will have to be spanned by overpasses several kilometers long.

We met several sailing-boats making their way downriver along the bank, where the current is considerably less strong. The waves and the headwind sent spray whipping across our boat, and we withdrew to the shelter of the cabin, where the mechanic served us hot tea.

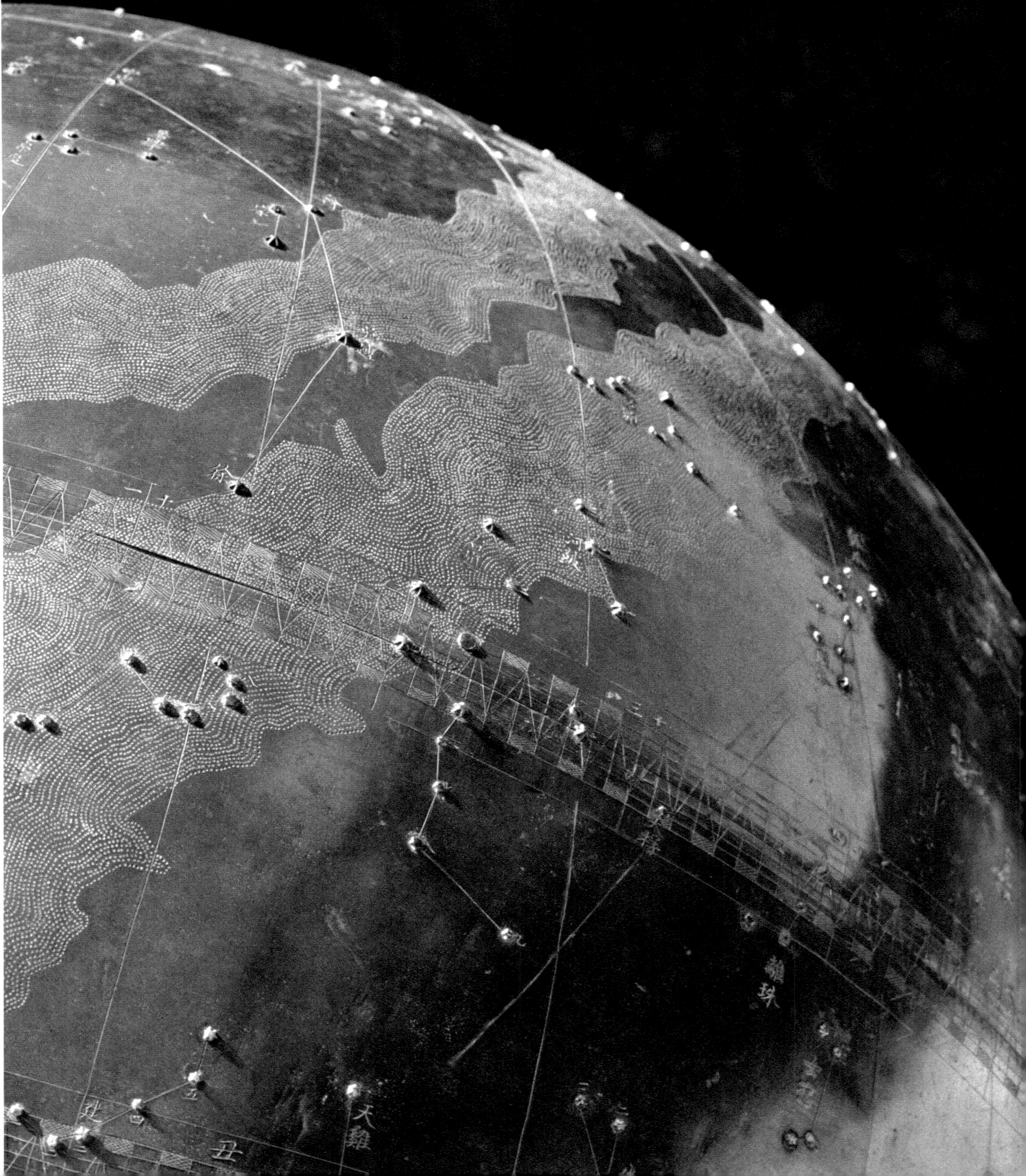

After two hours of sailing past iron, steel and chemical plants and factories, we once more tied up near the ferry station in Nanking.

35 *Porters with Nanking geese, Nanking.* A ferry boat has just come in. Crowds of passengers stream along the quay. Porters bring hundreds of geese ashore and deposit them on the quay.

36 *Scene in the Yi-hsiu silk-weaving Mill, Nanking.* The man at the loom is 59-year-old Liu Hua-ming, one of the oldest and most experienced brocade weavers in the mill. At the moment he is changing a spindle. He then carries on, controlling the pattern and the changes of colour, throwing the shuttle first from left to right, then from right to left; and between each throw he operates a foot pedal to open the "shed". Almost hidden from sight by the taut cords is the figure of Liu's assistant who (like his bespectacled colleague on the neighbouring loom on the right) sits among the threads and on the weaver's command operates the lines that control the actual pattern of the brocade. "Cloud brocades" from Nanking, Soochow and Hangchow were world-renowned as long ago as the Ming and Ching eras. The attraction of *yun chin,* or cloud brocade, lies in the portrayal of the clouds in the sky at sunset, using every conceivable shade of colour. This traditional speciality has been carried on in Nanking for centuries and is still being made today.

37 *A worker in the Nanking motor works.* We toured the Nanking motor car factory. Before 1949 the plant was a Kuomintang military workshop, maintaining and over-hauling military vehicles of all kinds. Since then it has been employed solely on making motor car parts. After 1952 the plant, which today employs 3,500 workers, was extended to cover an area of 80,000 square yards. 25-year-old Chen Mei-yih's job is to check the engines of lorries. Two types of engine are produced for the two-and-a-half-ton lorry, the 4-cylinder model of 50 h.p. and a 6-cylinder model of 70 h.p.

Nanking is famous for its beauty-spots, especially the Palace of the Celestial King dating from the time of the Taiping Rebellion, the Ming tombs, the Ling-hu Pagoda and the Hsuan-hu Lake. The pride of the younger generation are the university research institutes. Since coming to power, the Com-munist regime has paid a great deal of attention to these, their most urgent aim being the industrialization of the country. One of the most important preconditions for this is the technical training of a large number of qualified engineers.

We took a trip to the Purple Mountain and on the way visited the Sun Yat-sen mausoleum and the Ming tombs. After many twists and turns the road took us to the summit of the Purple Mountain, where China's largest observatory is located. Astronomic instruments from former times have been set up in the open among the buildings.

38 *Celestial globe of the Han Period, Nanking Observatory.* This celestial globe, which has a diameter of about a yard, was made two hundred years ago and is a copy of the original globe made by Chang Heng (A.D. 78—139).

In the case of a celestial globe the constellations are projected onto the sphere from the outside, so that the observer sees them as in a mirror. The portion visible in the picture shows the Milky Way, represented by many thousands of tiny engraved dots.

In Antiquity the Chinese grouped the stars into constellations and gave them names quite different from those used in the Mediterranean countries. According to the modern system, the centre of the picture is occupied by Aquila, part of which projects into the Milky Way and which the Chinese call "The River Drummer". Above Aquila there appears the minor constellation Sagitta and to the right, as a tightly bunched group of ten stars, Delphinus. In the top left hand corner are some isolated stars belonging to Hercules and under them stars of Serpens and the Shield. In the bottom left hand corner single stars can be made out which belong to Sagittarius, called by the Chinese "The Celestial Hen".

The graduated line running through Aquila represents the celestial equator in the position of the Modern Time. If it was present on the original model, it must have taken a different path, because of the precession of the equinoxes. In the bottom left hand corner can be seen a second band, the ecliptic. The lines running at right angles to the ecliptic and dividing the heavens into equal fields, meet at the pole of the ecliptic.

# Tsinan

济 南

In the south of the North Chinese lowlands, at the north-west edge of the Shantung mountain country, lies the city of Tsinan. It is the capital of the densely inhabited province of Shantung and an important railway junction connecting Peking with Nanking, and Shanghai and Tsingtao with the Northwest Provinces. North of the city the Yellow River, the Hwang Ho, China's second largest river, flows north-east. Another 120 miles further on, the Hwang Ho ends its 2,500-mile-long journey in the Inner Yellow Sea in the Gulf of Chihli. In the course of the last 3,000 years the Hwang Ho has changed its course at least seven times—some historical records say twenty-five times. At present, after flowing past the *north* of the Shantung mountain country, the river flows into the *Inner* Yellow Sea. In the 15th and 19th centuries, it ran for a long time *south* of the Shantung Mountains and thus came out into the *Outer* Yellow Sea. This change of course taken by the Hwang Ho would, if translated into European terms, correspond to moving the estuary of the Rhine from Holland to the Bay of Biarritz on the Franco-Spanish frontier.

After long periods of drought, the waters of the Hwang Ho can swell into roaring torrents of flood water in a very short time. In the 4,000 years since men first settled along the river banks, millions of people have perished because of the flooding of the Hwang Ho. In 1887 alone 900,000 men, women and children are reported to have lost their lives in the rushing waters of the great floods. But periods of extremely heavy rain are often followed by long periods of drought like that between 1876 and 1879, when thirteen million Chinese perished from the catastrophic effects. It is little wonder that the river is called "China's Sorrow".
The Hwang Ho has also been deliberately diverted when its embankments have been breached for defence purposes. Shortly before the end of the Ming Period, in 1642, the embankments were torn open near Kaifeng, in order that the ensuing floods should hold back the Manchu troops invading from the north. In 1938, as a defence against the advancing Japanese, the Kuomintang blew up the embankments in Honan Province, flooding an area of 20,000 square miles and causing the death of 800,000 people.

During our talks in the Tsinan Hotel I tried to persuade our guide, Mr. Hsiao Yin, that I really must make the trip to the Hwang Ho, although it was out-side the area for which my permit had been issued. I was told that my request would be referred to the competent agency and that moreover, only specially suitable four-wheel-drive vehicles could be used for the very difficult terrain.

We drove through the town in two Soviet-built, four-wheel-drive vehicles resembling jeeps. In the vehicle in front there were two officials, one of them a river maintenance engineer, who would be giving us technical information on the building of the Hwang Ho embankments. The rain came down in torrents. After 15 miles we turned east off the narrow approach road, both cars making their way very slowly forward through the incredibly thick and sticky mud, until we reached a long dyke that cut off the view of the low-lying country to the north. After some time we came to a second dyke, the south bank of the Hwang Ho. Before us lay the Yellow River, which at this point, curving from the north towards the east, forms a huge elbow. The level of this sluggish, yellow-brown water, on which a few sailing-boats were making for a jetty on this side of the river, was several yards above that of the land.

39 *The Hwang Ho, north of Tsinan, Shantung Province.* A group of men on the south bank are taking survey measurements. Their capes of rice straw protect them from the torrential rain. On the left of the picture can be seen one of the 32 syphons that provide the lower-lying land with water and with the mud which the water contains and which is so important for fertilising the ground.
The engineer told us about the extensive measures the government had been taking to try to tame the river's destructive power. In Shantung Province alone, through which the Hwang Ho flows for over 500 miles, over 300 million cubic yards of earth and, at particularly vulnerable points, 7 million cubic yards of rocks and stone had been used. In 1958, when unusually heavy rains burst the embankments at various points, one million people were mobilised in Shantung to close the breaches and seal off the flood waters.
During the winter, when the water level is low, an army of 200,000 labourers, supervised by 2,000 specialists, are permanently on the move to renew and repair the dykes.
At this time the water level of the Hwang Ho is normal, but the variations in the volume flowing at different seasons is colossal. For example, during the 1958 drought the flow was 200 cubic metres a second, and in the autumn of

that same year it was 22,000 cubic metres a second. Every cubic metre of Hwang Ho water is estimated to hold 76 lb of mud, part of which settles on the river bed. As a result of this deposit, the bed of the river gradually rises higher and higher, and with it the water level, so that the retaining dykes are continually having to be increased in height. The remainder of the mud is carried out into the Yellow Sea, pushing the delta a hundred yards further out every year. During high water periods the material carried into the Yellow Sea in one day is equivalent to a three-foot deep layer spread over an area of eight square miles.

40 *Convoy of sailing ships on the Hwang Ho north of Tsinan.* The mud along the river bank is indescribable. It is so thick, and one's shoes remain so firmly embedded in it, that one can hardly walk. We drove upriver along the dyke — to our left the raised-up Hwang Ho, to our right the low-lying land. We passed redoubts prepared for the protection of the labourers working on the dyke. We left the dyke towards evening and reached Tsinan as darkness fell.

Tsinan is not only a transshipment depot for agricultural products from the fertile Yellow River catchment area. Thanks to the deposits of coal and ore in the nearby Shantung Peninsula there has been industrial expansion in this area, lying as favourably as it does for traffic. The exploitation of these deposits has been particularly fostered by the Communists since they came to power and this has made Tsinan into a centre of heavy industry.
Heavy industry occupies a leading position with the textile industry — and Shantung is one of China's most important cotton producing areas. But in spite of these industries and a population of one million people, Tsinan, like most of the larger cities in the provinces, does not have the appearance of a purely industrial area. The foreign visitor gets the impression that every-day life still goes on in the old traditional Chinese fashion.

41 *Worker fishing in a canal, Tsinan.* From the bank of the Ta-min-hu, a small lake inside the town, I saw some men standing in the water doing something to lotus plants. Nearby there were some boats that are used to row tourists around the lake in fine weather and at my request an old man rowed us across the lake to the men.

42 *Lotus harvest in the Ta-min-hu, Tsinan.* Naked men were standing in the shallow water, feeling with their toes for the roots of the lotus plants, which were then loosened from the bed of the lake and brought up. The tubers, rich in vitamins and eaten as vegetables, were being carefully piled up in layers in a boat anchored nearby. The large leaves are used as packing material. The torrential rain, which had been falling all day, did not wet us, as the boat had a canvas awning.

43 *Schoolchildren in a Tsinan park.* Tsinan is a city of springs. In countless parks crystal-clear water gushes up from underground springs. Each spring has its name and a legend corresponding with its own historical background; our guide gave us an amusing account of some of them.

My efforts to visit Confucius' birthplace had had no success. It was a pity — the magnificent temple area, erected in Chufu to honour the great sage, was within easy reach of Tsinan. Then, too, the unusually poor weather, the continuous downpour and the gloomy outlook for the next few days ruined any chance of going up the Tai-shan, one of China's "five sacred mountains". The distant view from the summit, for which Tai-shan is particularly noted, would have interested me very much as a photographer. We made up our minds to leave Tsinan and took the night express back to Peking.

# Peking

北 京

"The town is built in the form of a square, entirely enclosed by earthen ramparts, ten paces thick and crowned with battlements. The whole design of the town displays the greatest regularity and the streets are for this reason so straight that he who enters by one of the gates and gazes straight ahead sees the opposite gate at the other end of the town. In the centre of Peking lies a palace, the largest ever seen, surrounded by stretches of park land and stately trees bearing different fruits. In the north, a bowshot from the palace, stands an earthwork fully a hundred paces in height." This was how Marco Polo described Imperial Peking and the "Forbidden City" lying in its centre at the end of the 13th century. The description still holds good today.

44 *The "Forbidden City" seen from Prospect Hill*. The view from Prospect Hill, made from the material excavated when the nearby artificial lakes were being created, takes the eye over the golden-gleaming, glazed roofs of the temples of the Imperial Palace, once the realm of monarchs, princes, eunuchs, mandarins and concubines, with a maze of harmoniously laid out halls, temples, pagodas and pavilions; with airy tiled courtyards, moats with elegantly curved bridges and many stone or bronze guardians in animal shapes.

45/46 *Animal Sentinels in the "Forbidden City"*. Animal statuary adorns the courtyards, alleys, temple gates and gardens of the "Forbidden City". Stylised tigers, lions, tortoises, elephants and fabulous beasts symbolise certain deeds and characteristics men hope to attain.

Surrounded by a dark red wall and a moat, this domain is still a fairy tale in wood and stone. Nowadays the "Forbidden City" is accessible to the Chinese people. Thousands stream along the broad avenues of the city of temples, where palaces and gates stand side by side, separated by harmoniously laid out squares with marble stairways and walls of dull red. The crowds queue up before the Gate of Heavenly Purity, the door behind which lay the imperial residence. The modern Chinese is fond of these wonderful palaces within his capital as places of interest that fill him with national pride.

47 *Girls of a Dance Group in the Forecourt of the "Forbidden City"*. In the forecourt of the "Forbidden City" hundreds of young people in festive costume are rehearsing for the coming celebrations to mark the fifteenth anniversary of the Chinese Revolution, waving coloured scarves in rhythmic unison.

48 *The "Temple of Heaven" in Peking*. A class of schoolchildren clearing weeds from the square before the "Temple of Heaven". This building is one of the loveliest of all those in the Chinese capital. Like most of the other unusual architectural marvels that give Peking its splendour and its imperial character, the "Temple of Heaven" dates from the Ming Dynasty. Peking, founded during the Yuan Dynasty (A.D. 1271—1368), rebuilt in the Ming Dynasty (A.D. 1368—1644) and extended during the Ching Dynasty (A.D. 1644—1911), is regarded as the classic example of the architectural art enshrined in imperial residences in old China.

49 *Chung-shan Park, west of the Imperial Palace, Peking*. The attractions of Peking include, in addition to the splendid temples, many green parks. Even the historians of bygone days sang the praises of Peking as the greatest garden-city in the world. The well-tended parks and gardens, with their romantically laid-out pools, bridges and ancient trees, still provide a breath of the exotic and colourful life of old China.

Within old Peking's historic walls, too, much remains of the past. True, the carnival atmosphere and noisy, bustling trade have disappeared, along with the dust and the garbage. China's capital is now scrupulously clean. Much of the old romantic picturesqueness, the warmth and the life, have also gone. But the visitor who cares to wander through some of the thousands of narrow alleys can still see in the yards of the houses the noisy intimacy of Chinese family life. Or he can enjoy the cheerful confusion of the stalls in the bazaars, where crockery, writing materials, lamps, pottery, bicycles, furs, shoes, silks and mountains of cakes and sweets are offered for sale. Or perhaps he will prefer to indulge the collector's passion in the antique shops.

Outside the gates of the city to the east extends Peking's industrial area, with strings of working-class housing estates stretching as far as the eye can see, with parks, schools, kindergartens, cinemas, club buildings to relieve the monotony. The area to the west is principally devoted to government buildings.

## 44

53

52

50 *Students of the Peking School of Physical Training.* The School of Physical Training lies west of the city, and has 66 open-air sports grounds of various types in an area of 150 acres. Some of the buildings provide accommodation for the 1,500 male and female students. There are also enormous halls containing running tracks and spaces for training in the long jump and in pole vaulting, in putting the shot, gymnastics and other disciplines; and there are also gigantic indoor swimming pools.

According to a recent newspaper report, the 23-year-old Chui Lin set up a new national and world record time of 13.5 seconds for the 110 metres hurdles. In the Wuhan Stadium, another Chinese, Ni Chih-hin, achieved 2.25 metres in the high jump. Another report said that the Chinese sprinter Chen Chia-chuan had equalled the world record for the 100 metres in a time of 10 seconds. These achievements were not recognised by the IAAF because China is not a member. Even if the performances of Chinese athletes are as yet inferior to those of Western athletes, further outstanding performances can probably be expected from China in the near future.

Peking is the cultural centre of China and the seat of the Chinese Academy of Science, the country's foremost research institute. In addition to Peking University and its Technical High School, the city contains further colleges and scientific institutes of national importance.

51 *Classroom in the Yi-hsueh-yuan Medical School, Peking.* The Yi-hsueh-yuan Medical School, comprising six hospitals with 2,400 beds, has 3,000 Chinese students. A small number of the students come from abroad, from Indonesia, Ceylon, Vietnam, Nepal, Cameroon and Albania. The training lasts six years. Most Chinese students receive a monthly grant of 15 yuan, from which they have to pay the cost of books and clothes.

Ever since the Communists came to power there have been repeated attempts to change the character of the Peking Opera. The old social standards underlying the traditional operas came under attack and censorship was occasionally imposed, "in order to separate the feudal chaff from the democratic wheat". But despite these measures the popularity of the classical Peking Opera remained undiminished. Even today, every child knows the heroes of such classical operas as "The Three Raids on Chu Village", "The Three Kingdoms" and "The Robbers of Liang-shan Moor".

52 *Scene from the "The Three Raids on Chu Village", performed by No. 2 Group of the Peking Opera.* The audiences are completely gripped by these performances and are ecstatic when one of their favourite performers pulls off a particularly difficult piece of business. This grandiose interweaving of musical drama, ballet and acrobatics, perfected down to the last movement, and the richness of invention and unrestrained splendour, combine to cast a spell on the audience that no Chinese can escape.

The political leaders are trying to bring about a change in this. "The place of emperors, princes, generals, monks, concubines and good and evil spirits is to be taken by the heroes of socialist reality. The themes of the 'modern Chinese opera' are to be taken from the history of the revolutionary struggle and are to reflect the conflict between the old and new ideologies in our society." These words were contained in an official commentary dealing with questions arising from the transformation of the classical opera, which, it said, "has no longer to serve the demands of aesthetic pleasure but the requirements of political indoctrination".

53 *Scene from "The East is Red", given on the 15th Anniversary of the Chinese Revolution.* This opera had its first performance in Peking on the fifteenth anniversary of the Communists' coming to power. More than 2,000 players presented the events of the Chinese Revolution in six scenes with an incredible display of scenic and sound effects.

Later, I was invited to see the same opera in Wuhan, where a cast of 600 took part. In the final scene, Mao Tse-tung's picture appeared on a bright red background. The actors turned their backs to the audience and made obeisance to his picture, while a great choir broke out into the final chorus of "Beloved Father Mao, the sun in our hearts, your light shines forth upon us whatever we do, you are with us wherever our steps may lead".

The "Hsin-chiao" Hotel, in which we were accommodated during our stay in Peking, is filled with a decidedly cosmopolitan atmosphere. Representatives of every continent are here, groups of foreign Communists, competitors in every kind of sport, ballet groups from neighbouring friendly countries, foreign journalists and photographers and groups of business men from Eastern and Western Europe.

54 *The Great People's Hall, Peking*. The great receptions for foreign statesmen visiting Peking or the mass demonstrations for special occasions—this one is in celebration of the tenth anniversary of the Afro-Asiatic Bandung Conference—are held in the Great People's Hall on Tien-an-men Square. The assembly hall, also used for meetings of the National People's Congress, China's "People's Democratic Parliament", can seat 10,000 people.

The preparations for the celebrations on 1st October 1964, the fifteenth anniversary of the founding of the Chinese People's Republic, began well in advance. The monumental buildings on Tien-an-men Square and the Changan Boulevard were decorated with flags, and countless banners were stretched above the broad avenue on which the parade was to take place. The street lamps were freshly painted and new light-bulbs were put in.

55 *Sunrise over Changan Boulevard at Tien-an-men, the "Gate of Heavenly Peace"*. With this picture in mind, I took a taxi to Changan Boulevard at 5 a.m. I found a small platform in the middle of the boulevard near Tien-an-men Square, a very suitable place for setting up my tripod and camera. I had just lined up the viewfinder on the point at which I had worked out that the sun would rise, when a policeman came up and stood by my side, gazing at me in embarrassment. It was a traffic policeman and I had taken his platform!
I hastily removed my equipment. There was still time to set it up again before the sun rose. The scanty traffic was beginning to increase, but scarcely anyone gave a second glance to what I was doing.

On the eve of 1st October, the anniversary of the founding of the Chinese People's Republic, the foreign visitors to Peking and a further five thousand guests were invited to a banquet in the festival hall of the Great People's Hall. Every nation and every colour were represented around the five hundred massive, circular tables laden with every kind of delicacy. Serious blond Scan-

dinavians were seated next to adventurous-looking Cuban revolutionaries; African girl students from Rhodesia and Tanzania in yellow robes were next to Pakistanis in sober black. In the gallery three bands took it in turns to play military marches and Chinese folk music. Fanfares and dazzling arc-lights heralded the arrival of the governmental leaders and, to the accompaniment of frenetic applause, Mao Tse-tung appeared with guests of honour from Asia, Africa and Europe, followed by Liu Shao-chi, the President of China, Chou En-lai, the Premier, and other high-ranking dignitaries.
Special tables had been reserved for them in front of the platform. The placings at these tables of honour revealed the varying esteem accorded to the guests. African dignitaries and Asiatic ministers were particularly courted. After Mao Tse-tung, the man who received the greatest applause was President Liu Shao-chi, who welcomed the guests and made the main speech of the evening. The banquet went on for two hours, constantly interrupted by toasts, for each one of which the five thousand guests rose to their feet.

The stream of would-be spectators of the parade on the 1st October began in the early hours. They poured into the city centre from all quarters, a flow of humanity making for Tien-an-men Square in unorganised groups with bag and baggage, marching in disciplined order to music and drums, with forests of red flags and banners, seas of paper flowers and coloured ribbons, on foot or in buses and lorries. The march-past went on for hours, until at last a million people were assembled.

Precisely at 10 o'clock a military band strikes up and Mao Tse-tung appears on the platform on the Gate of Heavenly Peace, to be greeted by an indescribable roar of sound from hundreds of thousands of spectators. The 1st October parade begins.

56 *Mao Tse-tung and his close associates and guests of honour take the salute at the 1st October Parade*. Thousands, tens of thousands, hundreds of thousands march past Mao Tse-tung in a never-ending procession, bands, athletic groups, women gymnasts, floats bearing huge models of industrial or agricultural equipment or models of cars, tractors, harvesters, locomotives and drilling rigs. Other lorries carry groups, frozen into immobility in acrobatic poses, depict-

56

57

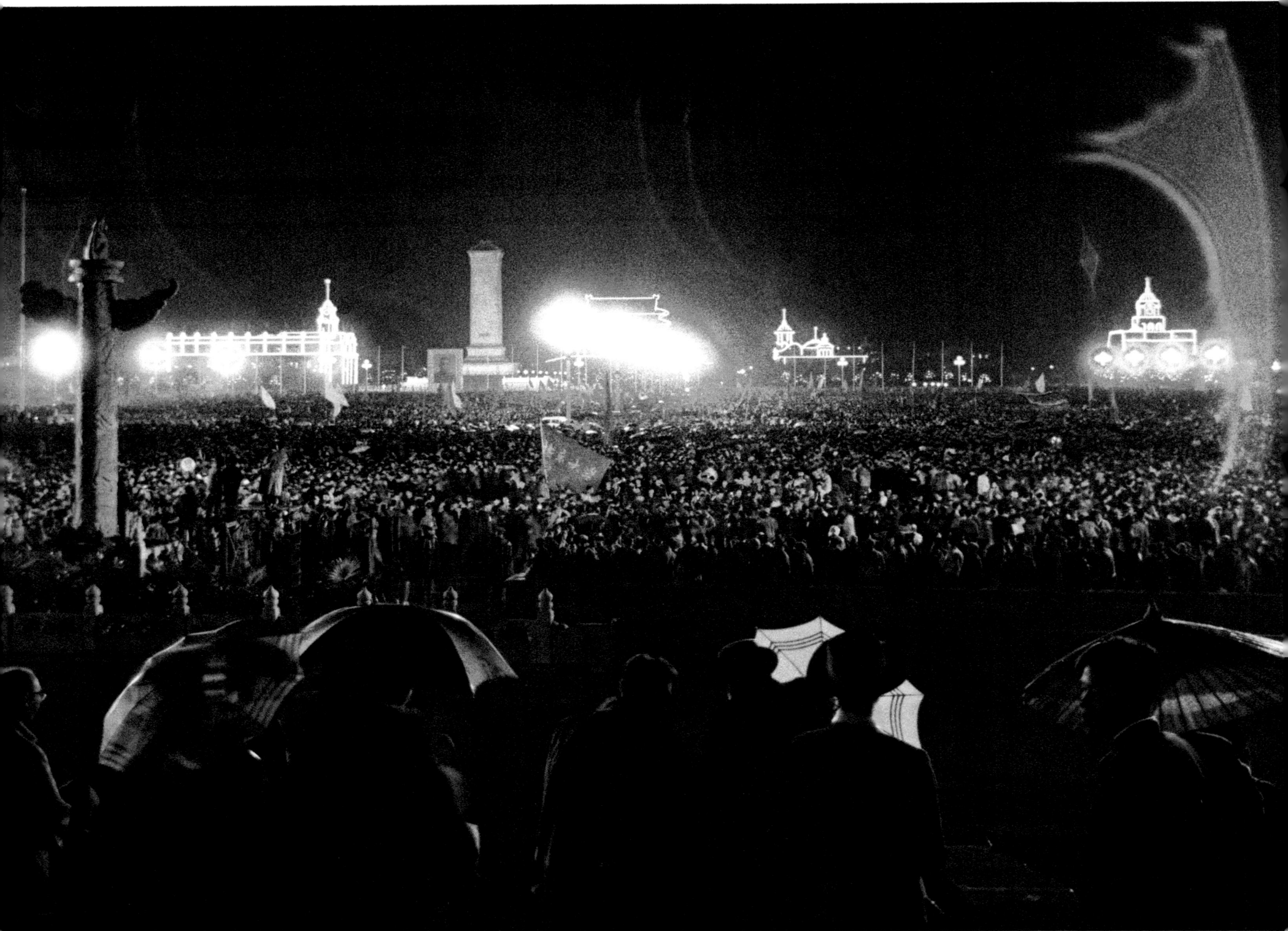

62

61

ing episodes from the revolutionary struggle. Detachments of the People's Militia, armed with rifles and bazookas, march smartly past.

57 *A Company of a People's Militia Division during the Parade.*

58 *Young Pioneers in the Parade.* Groups of children wave wreaths of paper flowers. The young demonstrators are grouped by colours, giving the impression of a moving carpet of flowers. On the square in front of the platform thousands of balloons are released on the word of command. They sail away between the scarlet painted lamps above the square, from which hang gigantic banners wishing long life to Mao Tse-tung.

59 *High school students in the Parade.* High school and university students and workers chant in unison. When they arrive in front of the platform, their excitement rises to fever pitch; everyone wants to catch a glimpse of Mao.

60 *The 1st October Parade.* Unfortunately, I was not placed as high up as I should have liked for taking my pictures. So I held the Leica at arm's length over my head, opened the shutter for an extremely long exposure time and as a result I got this unusual shot of the waves of parading masses.

61 *Illuminations on Tien-an-men Square, 1st October.* After the firework display, hundreds of thousands of people stay behind in Tien-an-men Square. It begins to rain and umbrellas go up. (The strange shapes in this picture were caused by raindrops on the lens of the camera.)

62 *Group of Sword-dancers in ancient costume. Tien-an-men Square. (In the background, the Great People's Hall.)*
The night scene on the vast square in front of the Tien-an-men is like a turbulent carnival. Here and there all over the square people are standing in circles around groups presenting artistic and acrobatic skills from all parts of China. If a foreigner approaches, the people open the ring to make room for him: they applaud him loudly and smilingly offer him a seat. Members of non-Chinese racial groups from West China show their local dances in magnificent costumes. One group of people wearing false "Castro

beards" and waving red flags present a dance symbolising the friendship between Cuba and China.

The rain is falling more heavily, cooling down the high spirits. More and more spectators make for home. The gaiety and lightheartedness die away and the groups gradually break up. The 1st October celebrations are coming to an end earlier than previous years.

# Why China Went Red    *by Edgar Snow*

When Marx's stirring call to arms first began to be read by young people in China after the First World War, they did not see in it an analysis of conditions in Europe of February, 1848, but a true description of their own immediate environment.

"The modern labourer, instead of rising with the progress of industry, sinks deeper and deeper below the existence of his own class", said Marx. In the United States relatively civilized labour legislation is scarcely a generation old. In China, with its child and female slave labour, its twelve- to fourteen-hour day, its starvation wages and the absence of any protection against sickness, injury, unemployment and old age, and no serious possibility of collective bargaining, why should people have questioned Marx's prophecies right down to 1949—the year of the founding of the People's Republic?

Long before the beginning of the Second World War, the old security under the Chinese clan-family and guild systems had collapsed and the have-not was literally worth no more than his price tag, purely "as a means of production". Behind the defenceless position of labour lay, of course, the disintegration of a traditional society based on a backward rural economy and handicraft production, both bankrupted by the impact of modern competition in markets dominated by Western imperialism. Capital levies in the form of ever-rising taxes (sometimes collected sixty years in advance), usurious interest rates, and the consistent plunder of public revenues by thieving bureaucrats and militarists, had, by the twenties and thirties, reduced the solvent land-owning tillers to a minority. Aided by famine and war, this ruined economy threw millions of "surplus" sons and daughters of degraded peasant families onto the swollen labour market of unemployed.

It required no sharp intuition to comprehend why, in a country where child workers of ten or twelve were often locked up at night, to sleep in rags beneath the machines they operated by day, the Communist Manifesto was read as gospel. Nor need one ponder why Chinese who met Western democracy only in its role of foreign policemen, defending "rights and interests" seized by violence in China, could readily accept at full face value Marx's scornful denunciations of its hypocrisy.

China was never a complete colony; rivalries among the European powers and Japan prevented any one power from becoming dominant. But China was treated as the inferior of all and was the responsibility of none. Any foreigner in the "treaty ports"—even a drunken bum—was superior to the most virtuous Chinese; to be treated as inferiors in their own country rankled for many years.

Thus nationalism, the passion to reassert semi-colonial China's ancient role as a great power, initially played a greater part in attracting literate Chinese to Marxism than it did in imperial Russia. In the West the Communist party had no comparable appeal. The Communist subservient to Stalin's infallibility had to learn to despise "national patriotism", substituting for it a religious "belief in a saviour abroad". He had to be essentially a mythomaniac—and often remained so even after he became an ex-Communist.

The programme which the Chinese Communist Party adopted soon after its founding called for a two-stage revolution, in accordance with Lenin's classical thesis for colonial and semicolonial countries. The first stage would complete the "bourgeois-democratic" revolution, with a united front of the progressive bourgeoisie, the working class and the peasantry led by the Communist party. It would end foreign imperialist oppression and win complete independence.

In rural China it would abolish rule by the landlord-gentry and equalize land ownership. In urban China it would nationalize the property of native "reactionary capitalists"* held to be collaborators of foreign imperialism. Only when these two aims were accomplished would the revolutionary power move on to lay the foundations for the second stage: building socialism. Programmatic aims of the "bourgeois-democratic" revolution, as thus defined, made a strong appeal even to Chinese nationalists. Within it, sentiments of patriotism, class wars, and international communism under Russian leadership were readily reconcilable. It must be remembered that at the outset the party founders' acceptance of Marxism coincided with direct Russian help to Dr. Sun Yat-sen in his struggle against foreign imperialism. The slogans of anticapitalist class war were also rendered more palatable because of antiforeign and nationalist sentiments. The small native bourgeoisie, including the great landlord linked with it, were, in truth, largely a collaborator class dependent on the imperialist powers, as events were to show. And it was simpler for the Chinese to believe in Moscow because Russia's foremost antagonists were just those Western colonial powers who were likewise the immediate enemies of independence movements all through Asia and Africa.

China's outstanding Communists were internationalists in ideology but no less national patriots than the Kuomintang "nationalists". They were not proletarians but for the most part came from the less than 5 per cent of China's millions who possessed some secondary or higher education.

Although Marx's version of all history as a perpetual class war was an innovation, his dialectical method echoed deep and ancient voices of Chinese thought. To Chinese intellectuals Marxist revolutionary dogma as applied to the modern world seemed, like the theory of dialectics itself, more new wine in Chinese bottles.

These men were also in a hurry. Their own experiences, combined with their study of European and American history, made them painfully aware of China's weakness and imminent peril of total effacement. In their search for a means of coping with complex problems of individual and national regeneration, young Chinese men and women of initiative and intelligence gravitated toward an authoritarian and revolutionary doctrine because other means had been tried and had failed, because they believed time

---

* Communist terminology distinguished between "reactionary" capitalists and "progressive" capitalists who helped modernize production. Quantitatively, the number of capitalists expropriated outright was small, but qualitatively it was high. As late as 1965 more than 100,000 "progressive capitalists" still received state subsidy in the form of 5 per cent annual dividends on their former property.

ruled out gradualism, and because Chinese history had repeatedly sanctioned revolution as a means of salvation.

The usual arguments against Communists as apostles of violence and destroyers of "individual freedom" had small relevance in China's *Realpolitik*. Freedom in the Western sense did not exist, and political change was still something attainable only by armed supremacy. Called upon to judge the Kuomintang seizure of power, few Chinese could have distinguished in it any ethical superiority over the attempts of the Communists, who openly sought power in the name of the "have-nots" at the expense of a minority of landlords, militarists, foreign treaty-port bankers and — during the Japanese occupation — outright imperialist conquerors.

Contrary to opinion held abroad, the Kuomintang never posed a clear moral alternative to the Communists but competed with them purely on a basis of efficient use of force. For educated youths joining the Communists, it was simply a matter of practical judgment whether their method was the only one which would provide a personal solution as well as quickly close the appalling industrial and scientific gaps between China and the advanced nations of the world. Those who became convinced of this in the early days made a discovery (which confounded all previous Marxist theory) that they could bring the "proletarian revolution" to power without urban or proletarian insurrections.

Mao Tse-tung's faith in the peasant as the main engine of social revolution developed from personal experience and was not shared by many Russians. Orthodox Marxists continued to believe that a Communist movement could not succeed without an advanced industrial proletariat as its main force. In the beginning the Chinese agreed. After their initial disasters (1927—1930) in urban insurrections, when the party was all but destroyed, they had no choice but to fall back on the rural areas. Real events thenceforth made the peasants virtually their sole material and mass support. Out of them came the strength which finally carried the Communists to national power, with minimum help from the heavily policed urban working class.

"Whoever wins the peasants will win China", Mao Tse-tung told me in Pao-an. "Whoever solves the land question will win the peasants."

The Reds never believed in land redistribution as an end in itself. But they saw that only by preliminary "land reform" could they get the peasants to join in a fighting alliance and later win their support for the main programme. Remaining the party of the proletariat in theory and doctrine, the Communist intellectuals became in practice the party of the poorer two-thirds of the peasantry whom the Kuomintang, wedded to its landlord supporters, could not claim to represent.

The reasons why the fire at first burned slowly in China were the very reasons why it could not be stamped out. Poor communications — lack of roads, railways and bridges — made it possible to create enclaves of armed struggle in the great spaces between the modern industrial centers dominated first by the Western powers, then by the Kuomintang, and lastly by the Japanese.

In the hinterland the Reds could offer leadership and objectives to almost universal rural discontent, agitate and awaken new ambitions, and build an army to fight for their goals.

When they actually carried out land reforms, eliminated some of the worst inequalities, turned the old gentry-ruled village hierarchy upside down, and took no personal profit for themselves, the have-not two-thirds of the peasants began to accept them and finally merged with them.

What was also novel and appealing to peasants who had never known the meaning of a political party was that they were actually sought as "members". Was it surprising that they began to think of the Communists as "our" party? It did not matter that the new peasant proprietors were later to bear the burdens not only of their liquidation as a class, but of both fighting the revolution and building socialism. What mattered was that it had been found that "peasants are people" and that they were wedded to the party—which replaced the vanished protection of the old clan-family system.

"The people are the water and the ruler is the boat", said the revered philosopher Hsun Tzu, twenty-two hundred years ago. "The water can support the boat but it can also sink it."

"We are the fish", said the modern Communist sons of Hsun Tzu, "and the people are the water of life to us. We do not ride over the people but swim with them", and of this they made slogans which the peasants understood.

In the contest between Chiang Kai-shek and Mao Tse-tung, time was decisive. Modern capitalism had begun more than a century late in China. As the nation reluctantly accepted the superiority of science and mechanized industry, intellectuals despaired of ever catching up by emulating the nineteenth-century West and using its agonizingly slow and painful method of "capital accumulation" through the private exploitation of labour and national resources. Even so, Chiang might have won against the Communists had they not received "providential" help from Japanese imperialism.

When Mao said that imperialism had "prepared the material as well as the moral conditions" for Communist victory, he spoke literal truth. It was not the Communists but Japanese imperialism whose deep penetration and occupation of urban China (1937–1945) crippled the bourgeoisie and destroyed Kuomintang morale. In doing so it opened the countryside to the proselytization and organization of the peasantry by the Communists. Japan's war, originally launched under the slogan "To eradicate communism in East Asia!" had the double effect of destroying Western colonial dominance in China and making it possible for Mao to arm the massive peasant fist of a renewed T'ai-p'ing Rebellion—this time led by Marxists, not Christians.

As early as 1936 I had summarized Mao Tse-tung's convictions in my book *Red Star over China:* Thus a great [Japanese] imperialist war, which is almost certain to assume the character of a world war, will release the forces that can bring to the Asiatic masses the arms, the training, the political experience, the freedom of organization, and the mortal weakening of the internal police, necessary for a revolutionary ascent to power.

In that sense Marx's prophecy that "capitalism digs its own grave" was fulfilled not only in Asia but also in Europe, where two great wars wrecked the old society. As George Kennan recently observed: "It was not Communist efforts which destroyed the old order in Europe itself in the thirties and forties and eventually delivered the Eastern half of the continent into Communist hands; it was Hitler who did this ... And, similarly, in East Asia, it was not Moscow, and least of all Washington, which really delivered China into the hands of the Communists; it was the Japanese."

Mao Tse-tung did not create or command the forces of Japanese imperialism but his understanding of them enabled him to seize leadership and control over the energies of nationalism and patriotic resistance, to win a sovereign victory for social revolution.

To understand where the Chinese have been, what they are doing now, and where they are going, it is necessary to know something more about the commanding place Mao Tse-tung held in their daily lives. He was the central personality in all internal struggles as well as in Red China's disputes with the USSR and its attitudes toward the USA and the West. He was also the least known and least accessible of all world leaders of his time. After Stalin's death, Peking recognized no living leader to equal Mao Tse-tung as a Marxist theoretician and ideologist. Unlike any Soviet Russian leader, he was for a whole generation the continuous and practically undisputed chieftain of a revolution. Like Tito, he won sovereign victory without Russian armed intervention and like Tito he contrived to retain his independence from Stalin's dictation. Unlike Tito, he was never called a traitor or a revisionist by Stalin—although in 1960 Soviet leaders began openly assailing him as a dogmatist. Under Mao the Chinese party evolved its own interpretations of Marxist theory, its own strategy and tactics, and its own idiom and "line" to fit Chinese conditions. Before the Sino-Soviet split, Mao's voluminous writings were acknowledged, even by Nikita Khrushchev, to contain "new contributions" to Marxist thought.

The nature of Peking's claim to ideological leadership—which was to become the basis for subsequent overt disputes with the Kremlin leaders over the "correct strategy" on the international front—was explicitly set forth as early as July, 1951, by Lu Ting-yi, propaganda chief and Politburo member.

He declared: "Mao Tse-tung's theory of the Chinese revolution is a new development of Marxism-Leninism in the revolution of the colonial and semicolonial countries ... Mao Tse-tung's theory of the Chinese revolution has significance not only for China and Asia—it is of universal significance for the world Communist movement. It is indeed a new contribution to the treasury of Marxism-Leninism ... The classic type of revolution in the imperialist countries is the October Revolution [of Russia]. The classic type of revolution in colonial and semicolonial countries is the Chinese revolution ... Study of [Mao's] theory will help ... achieve the liberation of all mankind."

Mao himself did not believe that he was indispensable. Anyone who has seen a little history made knows how impossible it is for one man to turn the wheel all by himself. Nor does one leader's death basically change all the infinitely complex forces which gave him power. The individual personality adds something to the mixture, but it takes a whole nation to produce a Stalin, a Hitler, a Gandhi, a Johnson or a Mao Tse-tung. Each man is the logical outcome of a long history which involves the whole world.

Of course the life of an outstanding person can tell us very much about a whole nation if we study the *people* all the way through, and do not just seek to deify a saint or burn a devil. The many days and nights I spent years ago questioning the unknown Mao Tse-tung about his youth and the experiences that made him a communist were far more important than an interview with him today. In Mao's case the early personal history happened to coincide with the feelings of personal frustration, injured national pride and patriotic dedication of a whole generation of revolutionary youths determined to remake China. And if Mao had been killed, as many of his comrades were, someone else would now be Mao, doing and saying many of the same things.

"Do not suppose", I wrote as my first impression of the hunted "Red-Bandit" of 1936, "that Mao Tse-tung could ever be the 'saviour' of China. There will never be any one 'saviour' of China. Yet undeniably you feel a certain force of destiny in him ... a solid elemental vitality. Whatever there is extraordinary about this man grows out of uncanny degree to which he synthesizes and expresses the urgent demands of the peasantry ... who are the vast majority of the Chinese people. If these demands and the movement which is pressing them forward are the dynamics which can regenerate China, then in this deeply historical sense Mao Tse-tung may possibly become a very great man."

Mao's life is largely the history of the Chinese Communist Party and the history of the party is Mao's life. His leadership was not to assume great national significance until after 1926, but in retrospect it is clear that his experience in organizing the peasant unions of his native province came to dominate his own thinking and, ultimately, the course of the revolution. Of all Mao's writings, probably none is more important for a student of history than his "Report on an Investigation into the Peasant Movement in Hunan", written in February, 1927, and urged upon the Politburo, together with proposals to change party policy, in the last days of the United Front.

Mao's report was the result of thirty-two days of travel in five counties of Hunan, starting in his native Hsiang-T'an. There he had gathered information to try to convince Ch'en Tu-hsiu, then secretary of the Communist party, that all the peasants of China were about to "rise like a tornado" of such force that "no power, however great, will be able to suppress it". He announced that the poor peasants of China were "the vanguard of the revolution". That was almost a heresy in the eyes of orthodox Marxists; only an industrial proletariat could be the vanguard of a social revolution.

Mao reported that "the poor peasants comprise 70 per cent of the rural population; the middle peasants, 20 per cent, the rich peasants and landlords, 10 per cent". What was more: the "enormous mass of the poor peasants are the backbone of the peasant associations". Also, "being the most revolutionary, the poor peasants have won the leadership ... This leadership of the poor peasants is absolutely necessary. Without the peasant there can be no revolution. Their general direction of the revolution has never been wrong."

Mao now and henceforth saw himself as their champion. Yet he and the revolution he led were far more complex than simple idealization of the poor. Mao was a realist; he believed in man and experience taught him that man consists of both what he is and what he could become. His sympathy for the downtrodden was genuine—more so than in any dynasty-builder of the past—yet he never forgot that the poor peasant hid beneath his ragged jacket the avaricious alter ego of the rich. Philosophically, he rejected idealism; yet he could discern the influence in his youth of a Western-educated Chinese idealist whose daughter he married—and who was executed by a Kuomintang general. Abroad, who thought of Mao as a romanticist? Yet in his formative years he was impressed by tales of folk heroes—warriors, statesmen, poets, scholars and patriots—and his own later poems compared himself and his comrades with those giants of old. In boyhood a chronic rebel against his father's harsh discipline, Mao nevertheless recognized that he had benefitted—"somewhat", he told me—from paternal severity. Later, he himself imposed far more exacting codes of behaviour on the whole nation.

His mother was a kindly woman, illiterate, and a devout Buddhist. As a Marxist, Mao came to regard all religion as "superstition". Yet the Communist party became in many ways the official Church of China, with Mao as its demigod.

A profound patriot, Mao dared to dream of restoring China to its ancient glory and dominance as the "central realm" of Asia. But he saw beyond chauvinism to the need for a world bigger than any nation and shared with Western teacher-prophets, Marx and Lenin, the sunlit and perhaps Utopian vision of a classless society of perfected men. Warrior, ideologist, poet, politician, teacher, commoner, peasant-intellectual—reason and passion all combined—Mao was a nationalist, Marxist, universalist, and—like the revolution he led—an all-Chinese phenomenon.

It was Mao's subtle complexity and his stubborn struggle to confront and reconcile the many contradictions of China in a "unity of opposites" that enabled him to triumph over the more parochial and far less imaginative concepts of Chiang Kai-shek's narrow nationalism. That task occupied Mao and the revolution for two decades. The *bouleversement* uprooted both those who fought against thorough-going social revolution and those who would settle for nothing less.

A founder-member of the Communist party in 1921, Mao was convinced by the example of the Russian revolution that only a complete upheaval could liberate China—and the world. Two years later Dr. Sun Yat-sen, father of the first republic, and founder of the Kuomintang (Nationalist) party, seemed to agree with Mao when he made a pact with Moscow which recognized that the overthrow of imperialism was necessary to achieve general emancipation. By 1927 the first Communist-Nationalist "united front" had established the National government at Nanking. In the same year Chiang Kai-shek repudiated the party alliance, to lead a counter-revolution which "beheaded" four-fifths of the Communist membership.

Driven to the hinterland, Mao Tse-tung then began the unorthodox peasant soviets based on guerilla strongholds in rural China. Chiang Kai-shek fought repeated "annihilation campaigns" to destroy the soviets in the central provinces, continuing his efforts even after Japan seized Manchuria, from 1931 to 1933. At great expenditure of lives and treasure the Generalissimo finally prevailed and drove the Red armies into a great retreat, in 1934 and 1935. Converting their defeat into a victorious epic now known as "the heroic Long March", the Communists crossed the wilderness of western China, under constant pursuit, and traversed 6,000 miles before they came to rest in a new sanctuary, in north-west China—to renew their struggle.

During that period Mao's supreme leadership of the party was established, never thereafter to be successfully challenged.

Meanwhile, Japan descended upon North China. Bidding for hegemony over the national-patriotic forces, the Communists proposed a truce in civil conflict while China united against Japan. Chiang Kai-shek continued his "annihilation" programme until, in 1936, he was arrested by his own deputy commander-in-chief, at Sian, and subsequently agreed to a second "united front" for joint resistance. During the war against Japan the Communists penetrated far behind enemy lines of occupation and organized peasant participation in guerilla operations on a vast scale. When the Nationalists fell back upon the unoccupied western and southern provinces, and began to rely upon American arms and money to build up a large army (which seldom fought), they lost effective control over the active resistance. By 1945 the Communists had increased their forces from 40,000 to more than 1,000,000—armed with weapons and materials captured from Japan and her Chinese puppets—while membership in the party reached 1,200,000 of whom some 90 per cent were under thirty years of age.

Efforts to form a "coalition government" to end the one-party Kuomintang dictatorship were mediated by the United States. When negotiations collapsed, in 1947, Chiang Kai-shek renewed offensive operations with 2,500,000 troops, against Communist irregulars who had no aircraft and practically no artillery. By 1949 Chiang's American-trained and American-equipped armies had fallen apart and in October of that year Mao Tse-tung was able to proclaim complete victory and inaugurate the People's Republic, with its capital at Peking.

What distinguished Mao from all previous Chinese leaders, with the exception of Sun Yat-sen, was that he did not mean merely to utilize the peasants in order to attain power and then drop them back into the mud. The ex-teacher proposed to end the misery of peasant life itself by lifting the people onto high levels of education and giving them access to the tools of a modern environment. To convince the peasants that by determined struggle they could own the land they tilled, and then to convert that sense of ownership into energetic participation in the mastery of their fate through the "construction of socialism" — such were the not inconsiderable ambitions which Mao and his followers pursued.

Long before Mao reached his seventy-second birthday, in 1965, he understood that those ambitions would never be fully realized in his own lifetime. Much less would he and his contemporaries live to see fulfilled the vision of a "completely selfless communist society" — in the words of Mao's designated successor, Liu Shao-ch'i.

In a rare interview with Mao Tse-tung in January, 1965, I asked him whether he believed the next generation, Chinese youth of today, would carry on the work of the revolution, toward communism.

Mao replied that he could not know and he doubted that anyone could be sure ... Of course he did not hope for counter-revolution but future events would be decided by future generations, and in accordance with conditions we could not foresee. From the long-range view, future generations ought to be more knowledgable than we are, just as men of the bourgeois-democratic era were more knowledgable than those of the feudal ages. Their judgment would prevail, not ours. The youth of today and those to come after them, would assess the work of the revolution in accordance with values of their own.

Mao's voice dropped away and he half closed his eyes. Man's condition on this earth, he noted, was changing with ever-increasing rapidity. A thousand years from now all of us (he smiled), even Marx, Engels and Lenin, would probably appear rather ridiculous ... And I do not think he meant to exclude any of his contemporaries among Western politicians.

# The Great Wall of China

長 城

After the exertions of the 1st October celebrations we left Peking the next day for Inner Mongolia. A taxi took us from the "Hsin-chiao" Hotel to the new railway station, where our considerable quantity of baggage was taken over by a porter. An escalator carried us into enormous, splendid halls with floors of highly polished tiles; and from there we went to the platform where the Peking-Huhehot-Paotow Express was waiting.

Punctually to the minute the long train rolled out of the station. Soon afterwards the conductress, a girl with long plaits, came to our compartment, bringing blankets, towels, slippers and some paper bags of green tea. She poured hot water into the teacups and left a huge thermos flask of hot water under the folding table by the window. In every "soft class" compartment there was a flowering pot plant standing on a white cloth on the window-shelf. The embroidered curtains, which I thought obscured too much of the view from the windows, gave the compartment a cosy atmosphere. We were thus made comfortable for the seventeen-hour journey, particularly since the dining-car was in the next coach.

63    *The Dining Car of the Peking-Huhehot-Paotow Express.*

Up to this point I had not dared to take any pictures from the train. Friends of mine who knew China had warned me even before I left Switzerland that this was forbidden, although one of them had managed to take photographs from a moving train, which he did in this manner. If he was alone in the compartment and saw something interesting, he would jump up, quickly close the door of the compartment, take the picture very fast and then immediately open the compartment door again. But this way of taking photographs was not for me, and I decided I should just have to resist temptation, even though the Chinese had never said anything to me about a ban on taking photographs. I have often regretted this since, because it made me miss many a chance of taking a good picture.

On the journey to the Great Wall, however, I could stand it no longer. If I missed the chance to take some photographs in this world-famous and historic spot, I should never get over it. When the train curved into the valley through which the Great Wall runs a little further north, I began to unpack all my Leicas and a number of lenses and laid them out on the window shelf.

Mr. Lin, my interpreter, was lying on his bunk buried in a paperback edition of the works of Mao Tse-tung. The train approached the Great Wall and I struggled to get the window down: but in vain. It was stuck.

As if it were the most normal thing in the world, I asked Mr. Lin if he would give me a hand. He immediately got down from his bunk and helped me, also as if it were the most natural thing in the world. Our combined efforts succeeded in getting the window open. When we went through tunnels and the smoke and soot began to seep into the compartment, Mr. Lin would join me in closing the window and opening it again afterwards. No word of admonition, nothing but a friendly smile and perfect courtesy. From that time on, the ban on photographing from moving trains did not exist. Whenever I felt like taking a picture while travelling by rail, I did so. Nobody ever prevented me from doing it, even when I had no interpreter as my escort.

64    *The Peking-Huhehot-Paotow Express before the Chu-yung-kwan Pass.*
The train went on through a series of curves towards the Chu-yung-kwan Pass. On some stretches of the line extra locomotives were attached in front and behind, but even so our speed was quite low. After passing through a broad tunnel we caught sight of part of the Great Wall. It was lost to view again and reappeared later, now on the right, now on the left of the valley. We finally reached the summit of the pass and after a few more miles the train made a stop at Ching-lung-chiao, the "Blue Dragon Bridge", where the railway pierces the Wall. (This and the following picture were taken during a subsequent motor car trip to the Great Wall.)

65    *The Great Wall near the Chu-yung-kwan Pass.* The Great Wall winds uphill and down dale like a colossal snake, now following the level margin of a mountain, now plunging suddenly into a gorge and then climbing up the hilly ranges on the other side, disappearing finally into the haze of the distant horizon.

It begins in the north-west tip of Kansu Province near the Chu-yung-kwan Pass in the northern marches of the Kilien-shan Mountains and runs south-east along the Hwang Ho towards Lanchow. Thereafter it crosses the southern Ordos Steppes, cuts across the endless sandy waste at the southern edge of the Gobi Desert, surmounts the 3,000-foot summit of Pa-ta-ling Moun-

63

64

tain and after countless winding turns reaches the east coast on the Gulf of Liaotung. Experts have calculated that the total length of the Great Wall, including overlaps and extensive stretches of double wall, is 3,000 miles. This would mean that in building the Wall—not counting the foundations —200 million cubic yards of earth and nearly 70 million cubic yards of stone were used.

66 *Part of the Great Wall near the Chu-yung-kwan Pass.* The Wall is about 21 feet thick at its base, and the parapet is some 18 feet from the ground. The ramparts, which at the steepest points surmount the Wall as flights of steps, are some 15 feet wide. At intervals of several hundred yards, watch-towers stand 18-20 feet above the ground.

The first northern frontier defences were begun in 300 B.C., in the era of the "Contending Kingdoms". China's central ruling house was powerless and innumerable feudal princes held unbridled sway within their own provinces. Merchants and peasant settlers were pushing forward into non-Chinese territories, especially towards the south, where the original inhabitants offered but little resistance. In the north, on the other hand, there was a series of running battles with Turko-Mongolian nomadic tribes. These tribes had first-class mounted armies and were not easy for the Chinese to deal with. Nevertheless the Chinese settlers continued their northward advance. The princes, in a permanent state of war with each other, were in no position to protect their peasants in the northern frontier areas, since their armies and mounted bands were needed for internal operations. Accordingly the idea grew up of building frontier walls that would at least protect the settlers against sudden incursions by the Northern tribes. These were the forerunners of the Great Wall.

The Wall itself was begun nearly a century later. The Tsin Dynasty (257 to 207 B.C.) had succeeded in unifying the Empire and establishing firm control from the centre. This entailed defending the Empire against attack from without. It was not difficult in the south, but things were different in the north. There the growing strength of the Tsin Dynasty had enabled them to push further and further northwards, driving back the nomadic inhabitants and depriving them of their best grazing land. The nomads were forced to

fight back. The tribes united into an empire under Hsiung-nu, an empire that gave birth to the Huns who later invaded Europe.

Hsiung-nu's empire was small but aggressive and dangerous. The Tsin Dynasty decided to maintain a large standing army on the northern frontiers of the Empire. At the same time they made a start, in 214 B.C., on renovating the existing border defences dating from the time of the "Contending Kingdoms" and began to build them up into an extensive and widespread defence system. Under enormous difficulties that cost the lives of innumerable forced labourers, the Great Wall grew into a magnificent piece of world-famous architecture.

The Great Wall retained its military and strategic importance in the centuries that followed, and was repaired and extended a number of times. It played an important role at the end of the 14th century, when the Mongols were driven out of China although the Ming Dynasty (1368–1644) could not conquer the erstwhile rulers of China in their home territory in Central Asia. Apart from its purely military function, the Wall had another and equally important purpose especially in peace time. Until a comparatively short time ago, it formed the permanent frontier between Chinese and non-Chinese. Against this frontier wall, just as against the city walls of the larger Chinese cities, thriving markets were held, at which the nomads bartered their wares for the products offered by the Chinese farmers.

Today the Great Wall is nothing more than a historical relic and the Chinese have long since pressed forward from Hopei, Shansi and Shensi, Honan and Shantung, into the great bend of the Hwang Ho, into the Ordos country and far westwards into Sinkiang.

We were already in Inner Mongolia and saw a beautiful sunset. After an excellent evening meal served in the dining-car of the Peking-Paotow Express, we lay down for a few hours' sleep. The sound of the "International", which came over the radios in all the compartments at 9 p.m. precisely, and the rhythm of the train wheels, rocked us to sleep.

# Huhehot

呼 和 浩 特

In the Inner Mongolian tableland, particularly in the central southern region, the character of both landscape and people has radically changed. The tented settlements of the nomads are no longer seen on the horizon and the Mongols' herds no longer move about in freedom on their grazing grounds. The smoking chimney stacks of numerous factories, brickworks and small iron and steel works signify the advent of a new era. The land has become Chinese and the Chinese are everywhere toiling with energy and zeal to change the age-old face of the country.

The area of Inner Mongolia is 540,000 square miles. Of the 12 million inhabitants, more than 9 million are Chinese. The Mongol population is estimated at 1,340,000 and the remainder are divided up into eight other nations, making the Mongols an absolute minority people.

Huhehot, the capital of the autonomous region of Inner Mongolia, has now taken on a mainly Chinese character in spite of its name, a reminder of its Mongolian origin. Nowadays one seldom comes across the typical Mongolian dress, the felt hat, the long silk robe tied with a coloured belt and the riding boots peeping out below. But here and there one sees in the streets a camel — or even a whole string of them — to remind us that we are not far from the Gobi Desert.

67 *Schoolboy in Mongolian costume in a Huhehot primary school*. The face most West Europeans would regard as "typically Mongol" is broad, round, flat and slant-eyed, but in Mongolia, as everywhere else, there are many different types. This expressive boy's head is that of a genuine Mongolian, yet he is by no means "typically Mongol".

68 *Outside the gate of the Siletcho Lamasery in Huhehot*. Even today very few foreigners are seen in Mongolia, so that when a foreign visitor does appear, he is at once surrounded by an inquisitive crowd. The people, among whom it is difficult to find a Mongolian face, are serious but by no means unfriendly. While they are always restrained, their curiosity is enormous. Just in front of this gate I had to change the film in my camera, and to make it easier to put the film in, I knelt down on the ground. The spectators all crowded around and formed a complete wall about me, their heads bent over me to

the extent that I was almost in darkness and could hardly see if the film was in properly.

69 *Lama in the Siletcho Lamasery, Huhehot*. There are still 27 lamas living in this 400-year-old lamasery. The seven oldest lamas, like this 69-year-old Tibetan, Lobsang-norbu, here seen looking at an old manuscript, spend all their time in the lamasery. The other lamas live in, but go out to work in the town every day. A few of them are doctors.

There are still a remarkable number of lamaseries and monks in Inner Mongolia, living frugally on alms from the people and the products of their own gardens. But their days appear to be numbered as Communist propaganda has more and more effect on the younger generation. The visitor who goes to see the temples and the monasteries in China finds it hard to overcome the feeling that what he is seeing is a purely tourist attraction. They no longer play the part in the life of the people that they used to play. The monks and priests told us again and again how generously the government were treating the religious communities. At last, we were told, the priests and monks were assured of a worthy existence. All the same, the expressions on the faces and in the eyes of the priests showed unspoken reproach and anxiety about their uncertain future. I shall never forget the melancholy expression on the face of Lama Lobsang-norbu as he bade me a cordial farewell.

70 *House front in the Old Quarter of Huhehot*. The houses are set back from the street so as to produce a rectangular forecourt, where domestic chores can be done in the open. It also serves as a playground for the children. As I approached one of these forecourts, the children took to their heels and disappeared into the houses, to stare through the windows to see what the foreign visitor was doing. I was particularly interested in the ornamentation of the walls of the old houses in the old quarter, but my guide had only a pitying smile for my enthusiasm. He would have preferred me to concentrate on photographing newly-built blocks of flats or modern public buildings.

71 *Grandfather and grandchild in a Huhehot Street*. The Huhehot streets are strikingly colourful. The squat blocks of houses are painted in a variety of colour,

## 67

70

69

every house and every shop having the doors and window-frames bright yellow, red, green or blue. This gave the place, in contrast to other Chinese towns, an appearance of cheerfulness, even of gaiety.

Our car had great difficulty in moving forward through the densely-packed streets. The cyclists had to push their machines through the crowds. The number of cycles in China has increased enormously in the last few years.

In the Mongolian National Museum, a gaily-flagged, imposing building, the stranger is shown the transformation that Inner Mongolia has undergone in the fifteen years since the founding of the Chinese People's Republic. The museum displays everything bearing on the impressive achievements—the reafforestation programme designed to prevent the desert's encroaching on arable land; the irrigation projects, especially in the bend of the Yellow River; the industrialization, particularly the show pieces in the great Paotow steel-works and the Huhehot rolling mill. But the visitor is told nothing of the history of the Mongol people. In a neglected corner of the museum is a model of the Iksao Meng mausoleum, the colossal edifice constructed by the Chinese at the place in the north-eastern territories where Ghengis Khan is supposed to have died.

72 *Scene in an Inner Mongolian wool mill, Huhehot.* This factory was built between 1958 and 1961. All the installations, the machines and the 13,000 spindles were manufactured in China. The 2,700 workers, who include Koreans, Manchus, Hui, Tahu and Tibetans, earn on an average about 50 yuan a month. The yearly production was given as two million yards of woollen material, 15,000 tons of knitting wool and 300,000 yards of plush. From what we saw of them these products appear to be of excellent quality. The visit to this plant, with its bright, modern work-rooms and efficient organization, made a lasting impression on us.

On the way to see a Mongolian kindergarten, for which we had had to give two hours' notice, we stopped for a while in the town. Surrounded by inquisitive lookers-on, I was about to take a photograph of an old man whose features had caught my attention. He had no objection, but then a young man,

presumably a Communist Party official, pushed his way through the crowd and gave me to understand, by his angry expression and the vigorous waving of his arms, that I was to stop photographing. I was astounded. This was the first time anyone had tried to prevent me from taking pictures. The bystanders were equally mystified. They could see nothing wrong in what I was doing. I indicated to the young man by gestures not only that I was annoyed but also that I had every intention of taking the old man's picture. But too late: the old man had quietly slipped away. Mr. Lin, my interpreter, who had clearly been highly embarrassed by this scene, calmed me down and we went back to the car.

When we arrived at the kindergarten, I asked the teacher, who was waiting on the playground to greet us, if I might take some pictures of the children at play in the open. Thereupon the children were marched out in long lines and called upon to sing a song of greeting. But what was this? The little Mongolians had been paraded in brand new Mongolian national dress and gleaming new boots, in some cases so much too big for them that they could hardly walk. Was this the reason why we had to give two hours' notice of our visit? The scene was highly diverting to watch, but at the same time I could not conceal my disappointment.

If one wants to meet Mongols in their original character as wandering herdsmen, one has to travel to the interior, to the immeasurably vast Inner Mongolian plateau. During my discussions of the itinerary in Peking I had particularly said it was essential for me to see not only Huhehot and its surroundings but also some place right off the beaten track. It was finally agreed that I should visit the region around Silinghot, a settlement in the district of the same name, lying some 300 miles by air north-east of Huhehot. There are one or two flights a week to Silinghot, from where the regular aircraft then flies on to Hailar on the farthest tip of north-east Inner Mongolia.

During our stay in Huhehot we had been escorted by Mr. Wu Yu-kang, a representative of the Chinese Ministry of Foreign Affairs. He expressed his intention of joining us on our excursion to Silinghot. He promised to get the plane tickets and to let us know first thing next morning if the weather conditions would allow us to make the flight.

# Silinghot

锡林浩特

Early in the morning we drove eastwards through Huhehot in a "Travel Service" car and after half an hour's drive reached the airport, where a twin-engined Soviet-made aircraft was waiting for us. Our baggage was simply put aboard the aircraft without being weighed, and as I knew from previous experience that Chinese airlines only allow 12 lb of hand baggage, I was expecting to have to pay a corresponding bill for excess baggage. I was surprised to find that I did not have to pay a single yuan extra and I assume that our high-ranking escort had arranged matters.

We took off from Huhehot in an Ilyushin 14 and were soon flying over deserted mountain areas, extensive regions of scree and gravel and broad, shallow valleys where there was not the slightest trace of vegetation to be seen. After about 50 minutes I saw what appeared to be a black line running across the landscape, dead straight for a long distance but then curving gently until it faded into the horizon. This was the Trans-Siberian Railway, which connects Peking with Ulan Bator, the capital of Outer Mongolia, and runs west from Irkutsk right across Siberia to Moscow.

Before we reached Silinghot the landscape had changed and was now a vast grassy steppe, ideal grazing land for the Mongolian herds. We saw Silinghot from afar, and soon afterwards the machine landed on the steppe and taxied to a tiny reception building.

We were met by two officials of the District Administration, Mr. Pai Shih-hu, a Chinese, and Mr. Wulichidelger, a Mongolian. They took us to the hotel in two Soviet-made jeeps, explaining the conditions and layout of the town and district of Silinghot.

Silinghot town, lying 2,700 feet above sea level, has a population of 26,000. Its local industries consist of small carpet factories, factories producing leather and other animal products and repair shops for cars and agricultural machinery. Apart from the usual schools there is an agricultural college, a veterinary station and a medical institute. In the centre of the small town there are two department stores and a cultural centre with a theatre and a bookshop. Buses run between the outlying settlements and lorries bring the local products, mainly wool, hides and skins, to be processed in Silinghot.

73 *Camel cart, a typical means of transport in Inner Mongolia.*

74 *Mongol children in a Silinghot primary school.* Even in Mongolian schools some of the children wear the red neckerchiefs of the Pioneers, showing them to be members of the Communist youth association. This school has 27 teachers for 550 children of all grades; and from the third year onwards instruction in the Chinese language is compulsory. By the end of the sixth year the Mongolian schoolchildren have learned 2,300 Chinese characters. Twice a year there are one-week courses in which the children from the second year onwards are given agricultural work to do. Each class has its own piece of land, which the children have to cultivate under the guidance of their teacher.

75 *Shoemaking shop in a Silinghot leather factory.* This room, in which several dozen men were making leather boots, was filled with the busy noise of industrious artisans. The 350 employees of this factory, which was established in 1954, turn out 25,000 pairs of boots a year, selling in the shops for 22 yuan a pair. All stages of boot production are carried out entirely by hand.

The district of Silinghot has an area of nearly 90,000 square miles and a population of 200,000. Agriculture is becoming increasingly important in Inner Mongolia, the chief crops being wheat, millet, maize and potatoes. There are also plans for cultivating large areas of the uncultivated steppe land for raising cattle.

We paid a visit to the "Ilita" Commune, one of Silinghot District's 122 People's Communes. The 1,150 inhabitants tend an area 70 miles long and 45 miles wide. The Commune's mounted militia, composed of 150 young men and women, were carrying out military exercises while we were there.

76/77 *Mounted People's Militia, the "Ilita" Commune, Silinghot District.* The Mongolian riders, some of them young women in splendid robes, came galloping along on their white horses. Fences had been set up and the riders were supposed to take them in pairs. Elsewhere, six-foot high targets had been put up and the riders fired at them as they rode past at full speed.

Mr. Pai Shih-hu and Mr. Wulichidelger told us that two hours' drive away the "Bayan-nor" Brigade, which belonged to the "Ilita" Commune, was holding its harvest festival. We drove north in the two Russian jeeps. After just

73

74

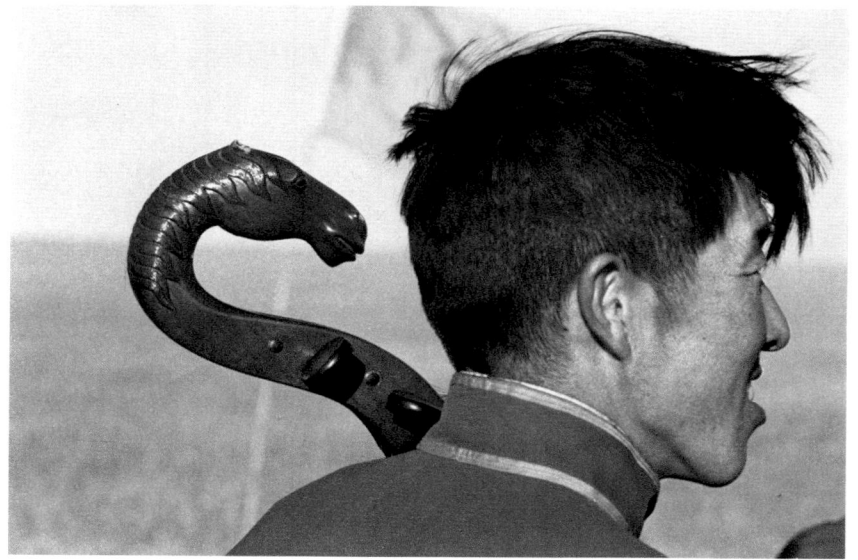

83

84

under an hour we left the dusty highroad. From now on we were running on hard steppe ground over broad rolling downs. In the distance we saw in a long depression white tents, carts, masses of people and a large number of tethered horses. When we arrived, the festival had already started and the traditional Mongolian wrestling matches were already in full swing.

78 *Spectators at the Harvest Festival of the "Bayan-nor" Brigade.* The spectators were sitting in their quilted costume around the wrestling ring, following the bouts with grave interest. The contestants were members of various neighbouring brigades. The sun was shining but there was an extraordinarily cold and piercing wind.

79 *One of the performers at the Harvest Festival.* Although this girl was wearing magnificent Mongolian national dress and sang Mongol folk songs during the singing and dancing performances given by the group, her face was more Chinese than Mongol in appearance. She was the best-looking of all the girls present.

80 *Mounted Mongols at the Harvest Festival.* Single spectators came riding up and joined the colourful throng. On the programme, in addition to the wrestling and the dancing and singing troupe, there were horse races and a kind of rodeo.

81/82 *Mongol musicians at the "Bayan-nor" Harvest Festival.* A band of six musicians accompanied the singers and dancers. The main instrument was the horse-fiddle (these often have the end of the fret-board carved into the shape of a horse's head). Mongol rhythms and melodies sound less strange to Western ears than Chinese music. The music seems to embody the hard, bare landscape and the raw Mongolian climate, and contains an element of melancholy reminiscent of the sadness of Russian folk music.

83 *Mongol women watching the wrestling at the Harvest Festival.* The harvest festival is the annual high spot in the lives of the Mongol herdsmen, who have very little other entertainment to look forward to. Every spectator wants to see everything. Men, women and children line the edges of the arena hour after

hour, despite the ceaseless onslaught of the icy wind. I was very glad to be able to borrow a heavy coat, which, though its clumsiness hampered my movements, protected me from the piercing cold.

84 *In the tent of the Chief of the "Bayan-nor" Brigade.* We were taken into a tent near the wrestling arena and plied with Mongolian hospitality. The Chief of the Brigade put a roasted sheep on the low table, around which we squatted crosslegged on the ground. He cut slices from the rich saddle and gave them to us with his fingers. There was also *airag,* fermented mare's milk, and *archi,* a very treacherous type of Mongolian spirit, to be tossed off Mongolian style, in one swallow. There was a good deal of smacking of lips and not much conversation.

After we had eaten our fill, our hosts answered our questions about the Brigade. This was a very time-consuming process, since the information had to come through two interpreters, one from Mongolian into Chinese and one from Chinese into English. The "Bayan-nor" Brigade consists of 158 people belonging to 39 families. They look after an area of 800 square miles, have 310 horses, 1,700 cattle and rather more than 14,000 sheep. Seven per cent of the livestock counts as privately owned. Every Mongol is entitled to his own horse, and this includes the children, who ride to school on Mongol ponies.

After the remains of the sheep had been carried away, there appeared a mountain of sweet cakes. The women busied themselves refilling our glasses with *archi.* I do not know if it was the unfortunate combination of fermented mare's milk, spirits, fatty meat, cakes and still more spirits that proved such a trial to my stomach, but I do know that the three days of our journey back to Peking after our leave-taking from these splendid people remain with me as an uncommonly unpleasant memory.

# Anshan—Shenyang—Fushun

鞍 山

We left Peking and shortly before midnight we went aboard the express that was to take us to the north-east provinces, to Manchuria. Our destination was Anshan, the centre of China's iron and steel industry, lying in Liaoning Province, south of the capital, Shenyang. Outside, it was pitch dark. The monotonous rattle of the coach kept us awake. I tried to order my thoughts and began to read some information on the history of Manchuria.

Manchuria, the once uninhabited land of vast, fertile plains, abundant forests and enormous mineral wealth, has always attracted its mighty northern neighbours. First it was Imperial Russia, who followed up her conquests in the Far East by trying to enrich herself at the expense of the utterly-defeated Chinese. Then the Japanese had the same idea. The Russo-Japanese War brought defeat to the Russians, who had to surrender their rights in Southern Manchuria by the Treaty of Portsmouth in 1905. In the decades that followed, the Japanese set about exploiting Manchuria, which they renamed Manchukuo. But their defeat in 1945 put an end to their ambitions and Soviet troops took Manchuria. Stalin got Chiang Kai-shek to sign agreements granting the Soviets long-term use of the Manchurian railway system and consenting to Soviet occupation of Port Arthur. The promised speedy withdrawal of Soviet forces after the end of the war was postponed again and again. Before Nationalist Chinese troops could reach the Manchurian towns, extensive dismantling of machine installations had taken place and the greater part of the available rolling stock had been removed to the Soviet Union.

When the Communists came to power in China, the Soviets had to surrender their remaining rights, which they did in 1950, after long-drawn-out negotiations. The Chinese, for their part, had to accept the fact that they would receive no compensation whatever for all the dismantling carried out by the Soviets.

In the bright early morning sunshine, we reached the southern regions of Liaoning Province. We were summoned to the dining-car, where a friendly waiter served us an excellent Western-style breakfast with two glasses of tea, ham and two eggs, four slices of bread, butter and marmalade—the whole thing costing 1.52 yuan a head. Around noon we reached Shenyang, where we changed for the journey to nearby Anshan.

85 *Blast Furnaces in the Anshan Iron and Steel Works.* The Anshan Iron and Steel Combine employs 100,000 workers and has 10 blast furnaces and 25 open-hearth furnaces. The complex comprises 40 different plants, including foundries, rolling mills and other branches of heavy industry.

86 *No. 10 Blast Furnace, Anshan Iron and Steel Works.* This blast furnace is tended twenty-four hours a day by three shifts, and is tapped nine times per day. Each tap produces 2,700 tons, making a yearly capacity of about 900,000 tons. We could not get figures of Anshan's total production, but reliable estimates put it at rather more than 4 million tons a year. The director of the Anshan Iron and Steel Combine told us of the destruction of much of the plant carried out by the Japanese before they withdrew, when they let molten iron cool in the furnaces. In 1947 Japanese engineers prophesied that it would take twenty years to rebuild the plant, and said it would be better to raze it to the ground and till the land and raise cattle on it. Some of this may have been exaggerated, but what the Communist government has done in rebuilding Manchuria's industrial potential is astounding.

From Anshan we went on to Shenyang, the capital of Liaoning Province. Shenyang is the most important industrial city in the north-east and is among the greatest centres of Chinese heavy industry. It contains large factories and plants for manufacturing heavy machinery, cable, textiles and various consumer goods.

87/88 *Soviet Memorial in front of Shenyang Station.* Beflagged lorries have brought large numbers of young people to Shenyang railway station to say goodbye to the secondary school children who are leaving to do their labour service out in the country. In the background stands an impressive memorial crowned with a tank. It was put up in memory of the Soviet soldiers who fell in the war against the Japanese, and commemorates those who "laid down their lives for Freedom and Independence, for the Honour and Victory of the Soviet Union".

89 *Main street in the centre of Shenyang.* Shenyang, with 3.3 million inhabitants, is the fourth biggest city in China after Shanghai, Peking and Tientsin. Five

94

93

wide roads lead from the circular city-centre to the business, industrial and residential districts, which lie separated from each other. The fronts of the houses and the style of the public buildings give unmistakable indication of the influence of the Japanese, who built the city-centre.

90 *Workshop in the Shenyang Heavy Industry Plant.* This factory employs 8,600 workers and produces heavy industrial machinery and installations—rolling mills for steel works, mining machinery, hydraulic presses and turbines.

91 *Scene in a workshop of Tool-making Plant No. 1, Shenyang.*

While we were visiting the factories in the north-east, the directors who showed us round told us frankly of the events and effects of the sensational step taken by the Soviets in the summer of 1960, when 1,400 Soviet specialists and advisers were called home overnight. Soviet scientific and technical aid in 250 different projects stopped at once. In the heavy machine plant in Shenyang, the Soviets were to have introduced a modern electro-welding process that would "enable heavy welding to be done with small welding outfits". This new method entailed radical changes in the manufacturing processes. When the Soviet engineers withdrew without warning, taking the blueprints with them, their contracts with the Chinese still had eighteen months to run, by which time the turnover would have been completed and the Chinese technicians trained. "The departure of the Soviet technicians brought about a very long period of lost production. Our engineers set about experimenting and trying to figure out how to carry on. It cost us months of hard work and desperate fumbling, months in which practically nothing could be produced."

We drove eastwards by car through the hilly landscape of Liaoning to the coal-mining centre of Fushun. The road runs for some distance immediately along the Hun River and here and there crosses the railway line on which a large part of the coal destined for the Anshan iron and steel combine is carried. Today this town, founded 2,000 years ago, has a population of 1.2 millions. The Russians initiated open-cast coal-mining in 1902, but it was the Japanese who really developed the mines during their occupation of the area from 1931

to 1945. During this period, they are estimated to have transported 200 million tons of coal to Japan.

92/93 *View of the West Pit, Fushun.* This open-cast mine is 4 miles long, nearly one mile wide and 675 feet deep and the coal seam is 120 to 360 feet thick. Holes are bored in the stepped sidewalls for the insertion of the explosive that breaks up the rock. Enormous mechanical shovels pile the material into the waggons of the waiting trains.

94 *End of a shift in the "Lung-feng" Coalmine, Fushun.* The coal seam being worked 1,800 feet down in the "Lung-feng" mine is 170 feet thick. There are in all 45 miles of horizontal shafts. 9,400 workers are employed in three shifts, and in 1963 the pit produced 1.7 million tons of coal.

95 *View of "East Road No. 1", Fushun.* The whole of the industrial area of Fushun, 10 miles long and 2½ miles wide, lies under a layer of soot and dust. Some of the workers' gloomy and seemingly never-ending housing estates bring back memories of the time the Japanese occupied the area. Still, new housing estates are being built and the workers here are paid the highest wages in China, so that the standard of living is correspondingly higher than in many other provinces.

# Changchun—Harbin

哈 尔 濱

After a seven-hour train journey we reached the capital of Kirin Province, Changchun. Our very arrival told us we were in China's motor-car metropolis, for we were met at the station by no less than three cars, one for our baggage, a second one for us and a third for our escorts from the "Travel Service", who took us to our hotel.

There was no getting out of a visit to "Motor Car Factory No. 1". In this factory, with its 21,000 workers, three types of vehicles are manufactured, a six-cylinder lorry, called the "Liberation", of 95, 110 and 210 h. p., a three-axled lorry and a saloon car. At the time of our visit only one shift was being worked, producing 80 lorries a day. We were not permitted to see the plant making the "Red Flag" saloon, as this plant, we were told, was being overhauled.

We drove along wide streets and splendid avenues to another quarter of the town, to pay a flying visit to the Changchun film studios. The staff here consists of 1,500 workers plus 95 actors and 35 actresses. The average monthly wage is 83 yuan, the highest pay for an actor being 197 yuan. Between 1949 and 1964 the studios made 200 films, 20 of them in Eastman, Agfa or Gevaert colour. Some of the equipment is imported and some made in the Shanghai optical workshops. The average cost of a full-length film in black and white is 250,000 yuan and of a colour film about 350,000 yuan.

The studios have also dubbed 550 foreign films, including films from Italy, France, England, West Germany, Denmark, Norway, Mexico and Japan. We would have liked to see the Chinese synchronised version of the Swiss film "Heidi", but there was unfortunately no copy available.

Six and a half hours away by train from Changchun lies the most northerly point in our travels, the town of Harbin. Here, as in other railway stations in Manchuria, the station name-board shows the name in both Cyrillic letters and Chinese characters. The Cyrillic spelling is a relic of the Soviet occupation after the Soviet forces liberated Northeast China from the Japanese. The older quarters of Harbin, too, have a decidedly Russian character. After the success of the Communist Revolution in Russia, Harbin became the centre for White Russian emigrés in the Far East, and more than 100,000 of them were living in the town during the 1920s.

96 *Russian Orthodox church in the centre of Harbin, Heilungkiang.* There are still said to be seven Russian Orthodox churches in Harbin. Their typical onion domes seem strangely out of place in a town with an almost completely Chinese population.

Modern Harbin is an important industrial city, a centre of machine manufacture, with factories making steam turbines, installations for power stations, both conventional and hydro-electric, railway rolling stock, precision tools and gauges, ball bearings, textile machinery and forestry implements. Between 1946 and today, the population has risen from 700,000 to nearly two million.

97 *On the bank of the Sungari River, Harbin.* The town lies on the southern bank of the Sungari River, which originates in the interior of Kirin Province. The river runs into the Amur River several hundred miles north-east of Harbin. The Amur, called the Heilungkiang by the Chinese, forms the frontier between China and the Soviet Union in the north-east tip of China for over six hundred miles. A hundred years ago Harbin was still a fishing village, from which it gets its name, which means in Manchurian "the place to dry fishing nets". Harbin does its origin credit.

For a particular delicacy we had been recommended to try "mandarin fish", caught in the Sungari and kept alive in tanks in the hotel restaurants. Accordingly we ordered this tasty fish at dinner, and the waiters were visibly pleased at our ordering their national dish. A large, splendidly garnished and excellently prepared "mandarin fish" duly arrived and put us in excellent spirits. I grasped the opportunity and asked Mr. Lin, my interpreter, if it would be possible to visit a hospital next day to get some pictures of a new-born baby. Mr. Lin was somewhat embarrassed and said nobody had ever asked for such a visit before, but he would do his best to arrange it.

Next morning Mr. Lin and Mr. Ting (of the "Travel Service") told me that I would be allowed to visit No. 1 Hospital of the Harbin Medical Institute. In front of the hospital we were met by the senior doctor, who took us to a reception room on the first floor, where we were requested to take

97

98

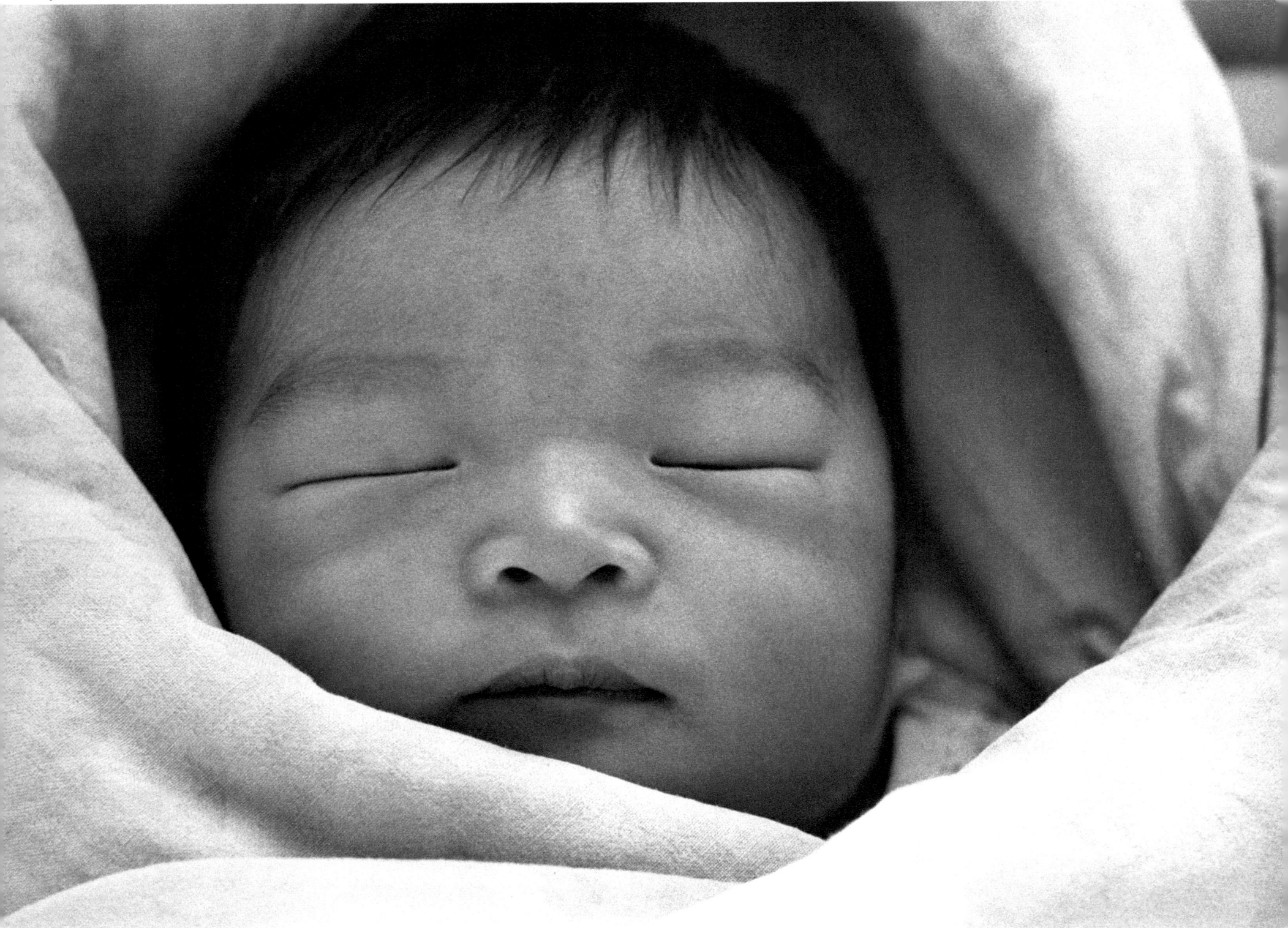

off our shoes and put on sandals that had been laid out for us. We were helped into white coats and had gauze masks tied round our mouths and noses and white caps put on our heads. In the next room we were requested to put on another white coat, this time a sterile one. Finally we entered a room in which there were a row of white cots, each containing an enchanting Chinese baby. My choice fell on a bouncing baby boy, who was sleeping peacefully.

98 *Wang Sien-chun, one day old.* The boy weighed nine pounds and was 22 inches long at birth. He was the first child of Mrs. Han Chieh-hsing, a 26-year-old kindergarten teacher. The father, Wang Chieh-hsing, was 29 and worked in the printing works of the Harbin Polytechnic High School.
On my second visit six months later, I called on the family at their home and presented the surprised parents with several photographs of their first-born.

Heilungkiang Province is China's greatest timber producing district. Harbin, the most important transportation point in the Northeast, sends timber by rail to all parts of China.

99 *On the railway bridge in the centre of Harbin.* Harbin is an important railway junction. Running west, the railway connects up with the Trans-Siberian Railway and to the east it runs as far as Vladivostok. In 1896 Peking gave Imperial Russia the concession for the building of this Manchurian connecting line and later agreed to the building of the Harbin-Shenyang-Port Arthur link, a stretch of railway that was completed in 1903.

The North-east's immense expanses of forest land, particularly the Hsingan and Changbai mountain regions, are among China's most important sources of timber. Three especially valuable products of the area are ginseng, fallow deer and sables. The ginseng and the deers' antlers are used in the production of medicines alleged to reinvigorate the body and restore lost youth. Sable furs are in great demand all over the world.

100 *Girl student at the North-east Forestry Institute, Harbin.* The 3,000 students of the Institute have the use of 70 different experimental laboratories. Large areas of forest land comprising jungle, cultivated forest land and felling areas have been allocated to the Institute for experimental research.
In addition to their scientific studies the students put in four hours a week on political instruction, the study of Marxism-Leninism and the works of Mao Tse-tung.
The foreign visitor to China soon notices that the fair sex's coiffure is of two kinds. Some wear attractively plaited pigtails and the others wear their hair cut short. We were told that the girls with the pigtails are as a rule unmarried, while those with the short hair have already "got their man".

101 *High-school students planting trees near Harbin.* One of the most important tasks in North-east China is reafforestation, intended both to prevent soil erosion and to foster soil conservation. In the middle 1950s the Chinese Minister of Forests announced that belts of woodland would be established for thousands of miles and that in twelve years China would be "one great green land". Millions were expended on this in overhasty mass operations during the "Great Leap" period. Today, however, the reafforestation programme is much more sane and realistic. Young people are brought in to help to realize it.

102 *Peasants ploughing near Harbin.* After the long, hard winter months the fallow land is being broken up, revealing the "black earth". This deep humus—the most fruitful in China—covers wide areas of the north-east, 80 million acres of fertile arable land. In spite of the long, severe winter and the subtropical summer that sets in immediately afterwards, the climate of the North Chinese lowlands is favourable to vegetation, and allows a growth period of from six to eight months.

The three north-east provinces of China, formerly called Manchuria, are still the industrial home of the Chinese nation. Although the population of 60 millions represents not even one-tenth of the total population of China, their share in the country's industrial potential is one-third: and there are political reasons for believing that the economic power of the three north-east provinces will rise even further.

# Loyang

洛 陽

"What's new?", I asked my interpreter, Mr. Lin, when we were woken up in the early hours by the news coming over the loudspeakers in the sleeping-car of the Harbin-Peking Express. Mr. Lin patiently waited until the news ended, got down from his bunk and told me calmly and matter-of-factly that it had just been announced that China had exploded her first atomic bomb. One could see satisfaction on the faces of our fellow-passengers in the dining-car, and one noticed that the newspaper vendors on the stations got rid of their papers faster than usual, but there was little visible sign of joy or enthusiasm. Even in Peking, where we arrived at noon and where we had expected to see mass demonstrations, all was as quiet as on any other day, as if China's first atom bomb was the most natural thing in the world.

A few days after our return from Harbin we set off again, this time for the south-west, through Hopei Province and Chengchow, the capital of Honan, to Loyang. The provinces of Shansi, Shensi and Honan were the birthplaces of the Chinese people and Chinese civilization. Here was for many years the economic heart of the Chinese unified state and the seat of powerful emperors; and here arose the old capitals, Sian and Loyang.

103/04 *Grottoes and Niches in the Lung-men Temples, Honan Province.* No far from Loyang, about 16 miles south of the town, lie the celebrated cave temples of Lung-men near the "Dragon Gate" on the Chi River. Hundreds of caves and niches have been cut into the face of the steep cliffs, every one containing statuettes, reliefs, sculptures or inscriptions, testifying to an age of belief and exaltation of spirit such as are seldom to be found today.

105 *The Fang-hsien Temple, Lung-men.* In a deep indentation in the cliff face towers the 50-foot-high figure of Buddha Vairocana, flanked by a Bodhisattva and the two guardians Lokapala and Dvarapala. Apart from these main figures there are countless other Buddhas of all sizes, the smallest only eight inches tall, in the "Grotto of the Hundred Thousand Buddhas".

Buddhism reached China in the early Han period, principally in the first century before Christ. The new faith did not gain a firm foothold until much later, now, in contrast to the first time, as a religious belief among the great mass of the people. This development was directly connected with the decline of the Chinese empire in the first five centuries A.D. After the collapse of the Han Dynasty there was a period of disruption and breaking-up, first the period of the Three Kingdoms, then the split between north and south and finally the centuries-long struggle for power by various groups in the south and the invasions by non-Chinese nomadic tribes, who established their alien rule in the north.

These events resulted in want, exploitation and oppression among the Chinese peasant masses. It was therefore not surprising that the country people who had suffered so much through the centuries embraced the new faith with such fervour. This was due not to the philosophical and spiritual value of Buddhism but to the new and revolutionary teaching, the gospel of life after death. At their next rebirth, all those who were now enslaving the people would be punished by being born into a miserable existence, but those who lived in misery would rise to a higher station in their next life. Buddhism offered the people consolation, hope and conviction.

However, it was not alone the profound distress among the people that contributed to the spread of Buddhism. The Turkoman and Mongol alien rulers also fostered it for their own purposes. This explains why the outstanding testimonies to ardent faith—these cave temples—are only to be found in the north of China and not in the south. Of the many foreign dynasties it was the Toba tribe, who took the Chinese name of Wei, that gave the strongest support to Buddhism. In the fifth century the power of their realm was growing, and with it the desire to have their own state religion. Buddhism suggested itself for a number of reasons, not least political. The tolerance enjoined by Buddhism suited the book of the alien rulers. The great mass of the people were devout in the faith, a factor which seemed to the Wei emperors particularly desirable, since they thought this would enable them to restrain the power of the strongest oppositional group, the Chinese gentry, the educated, land-owning class, devoted to Confucianism and occupying all the key positions in the traditional structure of officialdom.

This period represented the heyday of Buddhist culture in China. It gave birth to monumental works like Lung-men, which for sheer creative skill are comparable with the artistic wonders of the world, such as the Egyptian Pyramids or the ruined temples of Angkor.

*06/07* *Narrow street in the Old Quarter of Loyang.* In the picturesque, narrow, winding alleys of the old town centre of Loyang there is a colourful scene of bustling activity. In the two-storey houses with their wooden façades, mostly painted blue, reside the remaining privately-owned small businesses, where the most variegated assortment of commodities are offered, the trimmings required for ceremonial funerals, herbs for making medicines and drugs or aromatic pastes and ointments in white pots.

Modern Loyang has 600,000 inhabitants. New industries have sprung up in the outlying districts, the most important being Tractor Factory No. 1, employing 23,000 workers. But in the old city, once a flourishing Chinese cultural centre, time seems to have stood still. The key to understanding the backwardness of the provinces of Shensi, Shansi and Honan is to be found in the nature of the landscape. Yellowish-brown hills, barren and dreary, stretch as far as the eye can see. Unexpected ravines gaping in the level ground are full of ragged fissures, creating immense difficulties for both economy and traffic.

108 *Air photograph of the loess landscape on the border between Honan and Shensi.*
This photograph, taken south of Tungkwan, was lent to me by Count Wulf Diether zu Castell, who was flying as a pilot for the "Eurasia" air line between 1933 and 1936, when the Chinese internal air routes were being opened up. Count zu Castell's book "Flight in China", published by Atlantis Berlin in 1938 and long out of print, contained some outstanding air photographs. In the accompanying text the author described his experiences, one of which is given in the following extract and provides a picture of the difficult conditions ruling in China at the time:
"At this time 'Eurasia' had a special job on, transporting ten tons of bombs to the north-west provinces. One hot day, two of our machines, having unloaded our bombs in Lanchow, were on the way back to Loyang. I had heard a number of stories about an army of bandits, estimated at 10,000 to 40,000 strong, who were supposed to be roaming around in the vicinity of Loyang, but I had never believed them. I had flown over the area often enough during the past weeks and had never seen a solitary member of this legendary bandit army from the air.

"Our two machines were flying side by side over the last mountain range before reaching Loyang. When we were directly over the pass I was suddenly startled by a remarkable sight — a tremendously long column of people reaching almost to the horizon.

"Walking in single file, they moved along like a monstrous snake. To the right and left, villages were in flames, and the expropriated villagers were squatting on the bare hilltops waiting for the robbers to depart. For China's patient and hardworking peasants, famine, flood and bandits have always been among the inevitable and recurring disasters. As soon as the bandit army have stolen the last remaining goods and chattels of the poor, they move on. Then the burnt-out loess huts are built up again and the Chinese country dweller resumes the struggle to maintain his miserable existence until the next catastrophe once more robs him of all he has.

"As soon as I had got over my astonishment, I looked around for the second aircraft. I was horrified to discover that it had vanished. It was only then that I remembered that those people down there were by no means harmless — and it would not have been the first time one of our machines had been shot at. I immediately opened the throttle wide and I felt it would be advisable to gain some height, because I had begun to notice strange thumping noises in my aircraft.

"When I landed in Loyang I found several bullet-holes in my aircraft. Shortly after my arrival the second machine also landed. My companions told me that for some inexplicable reason they had suddenly begun to lose petrol shortly before flying over the pass... they had altered course and gone round the mountains so as to have some suitable terrain to land on if they had to. They had seen nothing of the bandit army. They were amazed when I showed them the bullet-holes in the wings of their aircraft, just below the petrol tank and providing the explanation for the loss of their petrol."

# Sian

西安

We spent the next twelve hours in a train, crossing the hilly loess country to Sian. We soon reached the point at which the railway approaches the Yellow River, near the San-men Dam. This dam has played an important role in the recent history of the Hwang Ho, "China's Sorrow", as the Yellow River is proverbially called.

As long as men remember, millions living in the Hwang Ho area have dreamed of the day when the vicious giant will be tamed, the colossus that ceaselessly sweeps along inconceivable quantities of loess mud from its drainage area. In the San-men narrows alone the river is said to have deposited anything up to 2,000 million tons of loess mud. Only 600 million tons of the soil are finally carried out to the Yellow Sea. The rest remains on the bed of the river, which is steadily rising. Thus the Hwang Ho represents a constant menace to the people, their homes and their fields.

The traditional rites intended to appease the dragon-god of the river brought no relief. Only by using modern technical methods might it be possible to achieve the desired objective. The first plans were worked out by American engineers, but the Kuomintang authorities had other interests at this time and it was the Communist government that finally got down to serious work on it. A tremendous plan for the systematic control of the Yellow River was worked out. The principal component of the plan was the building of the San-men Dam, which, backed up by 59 smaller dams in the upper reaches, was to hold back the water before it plunged into the broad eastern plains. When this dam had been completed, it was thought, the Yellow River would at last be tamed, its waters would be crystal-clear and the river would never again afflict the people of the surrounding area. Not only that; the control system would also supply 110 million kilowatts of electricity a year to the growing industries in the adjacent areas.

The mighty San-men Dam was completed in 1960, but there have been a number of official hints to suggest that things did not work out in practice as they had been imagined. Our request to be allowed to visit the dam was refused. It was clear from what officials said to us that the destructive natural forces at work in the world's greatest erosion area had been underestimated. If radical steps are not taken to prevent erosion in the area of the upper reaches of the river, obstruction of the sluices by mud or sand will be inevitable.

The journey by rail between Loyang and Sian was a very slow one, the train travelling uphill. The railway line runs through rugged, fissured, eroded country by way of Tungkwan, along the slopes of the Wu-tai-shan, the northernmost of the five sacred mountains, and through the broad river valley of the Wei-ho to Sian.

109 *Temple gate and market in the centre of Sian, Shensi*. Sian, China's oldest city, was for 900 years, with interruptions, the capital of the Chinese Empire. In this centre of culture Buddhist writings from India were translated into Chinese, celebrated painters and writers created masterpieces of Chinese art and Confucians, Buddhists, Christians, Jews and Muslims lived peacefully together. But the modern city is changing rapidly. Large stretches of the town wall, which once formed a massive rectangle around the centre of the town, have been pulled down. The regularly laid out streets, built centuries ago, are being widened. A traffic intersection has been built to open the roads to the city gates at the four points of the compass. Outside the gates there are modern suburbs with apartment blocks, schools and colleges, administration buildings and new industrial estates.

Sian is a cotton-processing centre, with many spinning and weaving mills, dye works, cloth-printing works and embroidery factories. There are 1.5 million inhabitants.

The Confucius temple, one of China's most beautiful temples, is now the site of Shensi Museum. It contains in the temple proper and its many inner courtyards a collection of over 30,000 *objets d'art*. A particularly impressive exhibit is the collection of enormous stone slabs, over six feet in height, on which 650,252 characters, comprising thirteen classical works of Chinese literature, have been exquisitely chiselled. Emperor Tang Wei-sung had these outstanding works of Chinese poetry, philosophy and geography carved in stone in A.D. 834 in order to preserve them for posterity.

110 *Stone rubbing of an inscription from the T'ang era*. Hand-made rubbings of the stone slabs, in museums, temples and grottoes, are on sale to the visitors. The

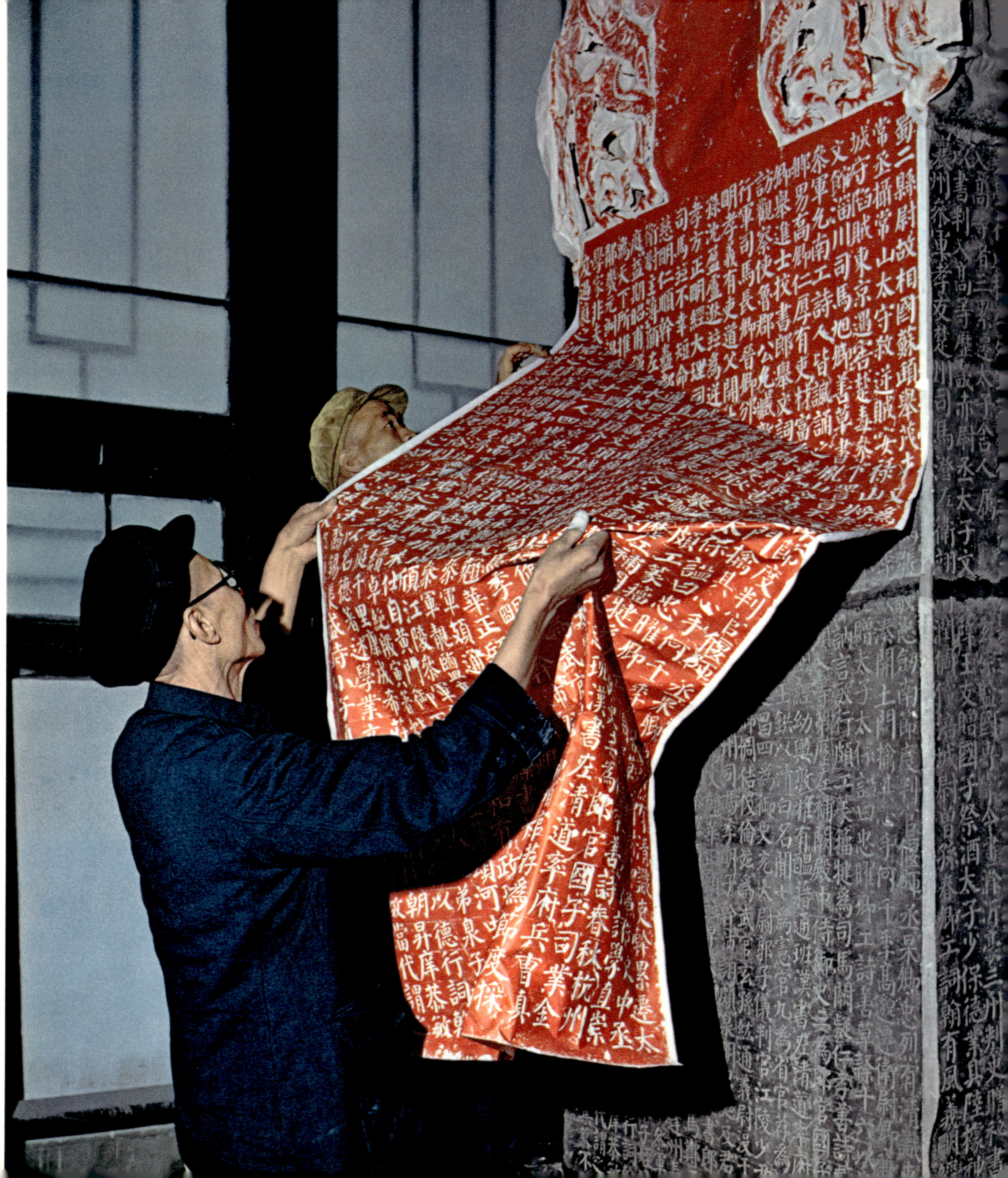

face of the slab is covered with a large sheet of paper, which is rubbed over with a swab dipped in red or black dye, after which the paper is carefully removed from the stone. This slab displays the written characters of a celebrated calligrapher of the T'ang era, in which the poet sings the praises of his great-grandfather.

In the Shensi museum we were shown the latest finds from the tomb of a princess, discovered not far from Sian. I tried my best to get permission to visit the site of the tomb, which lies some 50 miles west of Sian. After a good deal of stubborn argument on my part I was given permission to make the trip on the following day, but only on condition that I took no pictures between the town boundary and the site of the tomb.

The driver who took us to the tomb in a Russian-made car would have made a good racing driver. He covered the distance at terrific speed and when we came to villages or settlements he would put his hand on the horn and keep it there.

We were in a particularly interesting region, a place where, since time out of mind, the people have delved into the loess to make their homes. First of all the entrance is cut out of the soft loess and then the living quarters. If it is not possible to cut into the loess from the side of a ravine, a deep plot is cut out of the surface above and this later becomes a threshing floor. Around this cut-out area the various rooms are hollowed out of the loess. The "house" fronts are often painted blue, which gives the cave settlements a festive appearance. These loess caves are dry and durable, warm in winter and cool in summer. But they are susceptible to collapse through earthquakes and the floods that follow cloudbursts. It was a great pity we were not allowed to stop anywhere. I would very much have liked to take some photographs, because this road we were on was not just any old road in China, but the famous "Silk Road", along which wares from the Near East were taken to China as far back as the third century B.C. and along which Marco Polo travelled to Peking at the time of the Mongol Empire.

Our objective, when we reached it, lay directly at the side of the road, the pyramid-shaped tomb of Princess Yung Tai, the seventh daughter of the

T'ang Emperor Chung-tsung, who died at 17 years of age giving birth to her first child.

111 *Relief in the vault of the tomb of Princess Yung Tai*. Archaeologists from Sian began excavating in 1960. A corridor 80 yards long and four yards wide, containing niches and small chambers, leads to the interior. The walls and ceilings of the corridor and the chambers have painted frescoes. Unfortunately the majority of these have been painted over with glaring colours and the original motifs, in delicate pastel shades, can only be seen here and there. At the very end of the corridor is the narrow tomb, containing a cube composed of dark stone slabs engraved with splendid pictures and ornamentation.

A narrow road of soft, clayish soil took us to a mound at the foot of the hill where the tomb of the Empress Wu Tse-tien lies, still untouched. Around the hill are seventeen other tombs of princes, princesses, generals and ministers of this royal family of the T'ang Dynasty.

112/13 *Winged horse at the entrance to the avenue leading to the Mausoleum of Empress Wu Tse-tien*. An avenue flanked on both sides by pillars and stone figures of riders, horses, humans and ostriches, leads to a mound. At the end of the avenue, facing east, are two large stone lions and next to them ranks of praying figures in stone, whose heads have been knocked off. A path leads from the mound to Liang-shan Hill: and at the end of the path is the entrance to the mausoleum.

# Revolutionary China in Transition     *by Harry Hamm*

The Communists have been in power in China for nearly twenty years. Their victory over the Nationalists was largely based on the promise, which they made so vehemently, that they would accomplish a social revolution in China, establish law and order in a country plagued by war and unrest for years, and raise and consolidate the standard of living of the mass of the population. What has become of these objectives? Have the efforts of the revolutionary Communist élite been successful? Have those in power succeeded in winning all, or in part, the sympathy of the mass of the Chinese people?

It is not easy to answer all these questions. Communist propaganda gives a thoroughly biased and rosy picture. Opponents of the regime, on the other hand, tend to magnify the failures of a development or generalize from them. Anyone who wants to form a judgment based on personal observation finds himself up against difficulties. China is gigantic and has many facets. Circumstances and conditions vary from place to place. The temperament and mentality of the population in one region will be quite different from that in another. On top of this, the Chinese do not make it easy for the foreigner to get to the heart of the matter. He is forbidden to enter many parts of the country, perhaps even those which are most interesting. He is not allowed an insight into important institutions forming part of the apparatus of leadership. A dexterous propaganda machine that is not averse to manipulation threatens to lay a smoke screen in front of him or put him on the wrong track. But for all the courtesy and kindness of the individual Chinese, the main thing that is missing is the important element of natural human communication. The foreigner never makes a personal contact or finds himself in a situation in which sympathy can develop and ultimately lead to a frank exchange of views. An invisible wall always seems to slide in front of him, forming an insuperable obstacle. The reasons lie partly in the Chinese character, partly in the psychological effects of strict political control.

Consequently, many reservations are advisable when it comes to evaluating and judging the general situation in China. However, if we look at things objectively, we must admit that Communist policy has had some important successes. First and foremost the leadership has managed to give the country unity and a central power structure after years of disunity and degradation. As a natural consequence a strengthening of national self-confidence among the population is unmistakable. Simultaneously with the establishment of a central power, important prerequisites for an improved system of administration and the provision of necessities were created. The realisation that they are part of an integrated whole has penetrated the people's consciousness. In China today there is an extraordinary standard of social and physical security that was quite unknown before. Undeniable too are the government's successes in the field of primary education and hygiene. Finally, we must not forget that the higher status of China as a political power, which Peking has managed to create—never mind how—in the eyes of the world, fills every Chinese, whether Communist or not, with pride. China's awakening from a provincial backwater existence, the attention paid to the Chinese Communists' opinions and evaluations of international problems by the leaders of world politics, her rise as a dominant regional power in Asia and her entry into the circle of atomic powers, are all developments that have raised China's prestige; but they have also increased fears outside her frontiers. Both factors undoubtedly strengthen the Chinese people's feeling of solidarity.

The consolidation of a strong political central power and its consequences have created the essential conditions for bringing China out of its old, traditional and backward social structure, and paving the way for a higher economic, social and political order. Only a central power will be in the position to bring about those revolutionising changes in the traditional methods of production, the concept of society and the scale of values that are basic necessities for a sweeping renaissance. Here, three tasks seem to be urgent. First, a limitation of the large numbers of children, which are looked on as a blessing in every backward society, but preclude the possibility of rising to a higher form of social order. Second, to transform a society predominantly devoted to agriculture into one in which industry and commerce are in the ascendancy. In other words, agriculture must be encouraged until it can feed the growing population adequately and also set free capital—it can only come from agriculture—for the purchase of capital goods for industry to be built up. This capital may also eventually pay for the import of necessary foodstuffs or capital goods that cannot yet be produced in the country itself. Third, the traditional placing of a man in society according to the specific class, rank or educated élite he belonged to, or his connexions with those in power, must give way to the assessment of his personal abilities to fulfil a specific function within the new social structure to which China is aspiring. Whenever backward societies try to develop themselves, demographic, social and educational policies are the decisive factors. China is no exception to this rule. Has the leadership been successful in carrying out these elementary tasks?

*Every fourth person in the world is Chinese*

After even a brief stay in the big cities and major provinces the indescribable swarms of humanity begin to depress the foreign visitor. The towns are bursting at their seams. The giddy-making concentration of people in the fertile regions becomes terrifying. It almost looks as if every second Chinese is a child; wherever you look, wherever you go, a few children are always standing and gazing curiously, delightedly or shyly at the odd exotic "long nose". In short, the density of China has become a nightmare. However, the exact population figures remain a secret, as before. Even such a strictly controlled state as the Communist People's Republic, with its army of civil servants and officials, has scarcely been able to make any progress here. Today, as from time immemorial, you are referred to estimates. In the prevailing opinion of the experts, the population of China is about 700 million. In other words, every fourth person in the world is Chinese.

The figure of 700 million alone would not be so worrying; China is large, there are still vast empty spaces. Much more serious is the population increase. Experts have calculated that there will be 1,000 million Chinese in 1980; at the turn of the century there will be as many as 1,200 million. These are figures that automatically conjure up the frightening idea of a "yellow peril". Official circles in Peking once stated that the annual population increase was at least fifteen million. Now this high growth is certainly not mainly attributable to a higher birth rate. It is fairly safe to say that there are fewer new-born children in China today than at any time in the past. But the death rate has decreased considerably; it has fallen more than the birth rate. I was told in Peking that the average expectation of life of a Chinese was formerly about thirty years, whereas today it has jumped to fifty years.

That may be an exaggeration, but there is undoubtedly a grain of truth in this assertion. The death rate is lower than it was in the past because of two measures that were introduced by the regime with strict discipline—the first in the field of hygiene and the second in the sphere of medical care; they had impressive results. Already the cleanliness in the streets and residential districts of Chinese towns has become almost a by-word. The Communist cadres pay strict attention to the observation of the rules of hygiene. A network of medical institutions covers the country and is able to provide both remedies and prophylactic services on a far larger scale than before. The task then arose of controlling the consequent population increase in the only way that seemed possible—by developing a programme of birth control and family planning.

A Communist government comes up against quite insuperable difficulties when considering family planning. It must take into account Karl Marx's thesis according to which people could increase more rapidly than the basic food supplies expand only in a capitalist society in certain circumstances; a Communist, planned economy, on the other hand, would always be in a position to produce comparatively more than the population increase amounted to. In their early years in power, the Chinese Communists acted on this maxim. Every form of birth control was taboo. This attitude did not change until the gigantic efforts in the years of the "Great Leap Forward" turned out to be a fiasco. In that period between 1958 and 1961, the prevailing view was that there simply could not be too many hands to put into practice the splendid solutions that the leadership had prescribed as self-sacrificing stages on the road to the Communist paradise.

Millions upon millions were assembled into labour armies to dig canals and irrigation systems, erect dams or make steel by "do-it-yourself" methods. Under these circumstances, the idea of birth control must have seemed paradoxical. It was the vast setbacks to the "Great Leap" that first led to disillusion. From the beginning of 1962 the ways and means of introducing a suitable form of birth control suddenly became urgent again and family planning became an important item on the programme of the Communist leadership.

Today, three main ways are used to check the population increase in China: first, propaganda for late marriages, second, contraception and third, termination of pregnancy or sterilization. The campaign for late marriage is far and away at the head of all these efforts. It is the cornerstone of Communist family planning and gives the greatest promise of success because there are so many opportunities for influencing the people. After numerous conversations with officials in all parts of the country, I had the impression that an unwritten norm had been established by which, as far as possible, men should not marry until they were thirty, and women not until they were twenty-five. The advantages of late marriage are demonstrated through the usual media for explanation and instruction: talks on the radio, newspaper articles and pamphlets, mass meetings and school lessons. It looks as if the leadership has largely succeeded in convincing the young people at least that the principle of late marriage is to their own advantage and in the country's interest. The second feature of Chinese demographic policy culminates in the slogan: Produce fewer, but healthier children! The regime tries to convince married couples to keep their families as small as possible with almost the same arguments that are put forward when agitating for and explaining late marriage. Families with two, or at most three, children are considered the ideal.

But the reality is still far from this. The dream of large numbers of children as a laudable aim will not be eradicated among the people for a long time yet. Intensive propaganda for the use of contraceptives has not been able to change this much. Atavistic traditions, timidity and a sense of shame are deep-rooted. However, the efforts of Chinese politicians specialising in population, and particularly their willingness to learn from Japan's experiences, reveal that the problem of birth control is taken more and more seriously. In comparison with the propaganda for late marriage and family planning, agitation for abortion or sterilization is very little in evidence. Not only are the medical facilities for them virtually unavailable, but also they meet with the strongest psychologically conditioned opposition from the people. This leads us to the conclusion that the regime has by no means succeeded in compensating for the decrease in the death rate by a corresponding decrease in the birth rate. In terms of generations, the danger remains that the enormous increase in population is a threat to the stability of the nation. Even though considerable success in the field of family planning is obvious, it is not enough to give the leadership cause for excessive optimism.

*An economic policy on two legs*

The economic goals set by the regime give particular cause for scepticism. China is, and has been for many years, an agrarian country. Primarily, agriculture has to feed a rapidly increasing population, but at the same time it is the only source of finance for development. China wants to, and must, become an industrial nation, if backwardness and want are to be overcome. However, the necessary capital investment can only come from agriculture. The very fact that not even the food situation seems to be assured in China demonstrates how problematical the future is.

Rare indications from official circles reveal that an appreciable increase in the yields of the basic foodstuffs, rice and wheat, during recent years, has not proved possible. The last relatively reliable statistics from 1957 give a harvest of 185 million tons. In 1964 the harvest was reckoned at just under 190 million tons, a serious symptom, if we bear in mind that the population of China has increased by at least 100 million since 1957. Nevertheless, responsible officials of the planning authorities in the Chinese capital behave optimistically. Over and over again they point out that Japan was able to solve the feeding problem in much less favourable circumstances. Even if the farmers stuck to the existing cultivable area and were able to use the same intensive methods as the Japanese, a fourfold increase in the harvest would inevitably follow. But if they increased the cultivable area as much as the planners in Peking visualised, they would certainly manage not only to cover their own requirements, but also to export considerable amounts of cereals. "We have three times as much cultivable land per head of population as Japan. Moreover, we are in a position to enlarge our cultivable area by fifty per cent. The problem of our agrarian policy is not that we have too little land or that more cannot be produced from the existing cultivable area. Our real and only problem is how we can produce the national capital in order to achieve these greater yields in agriculture." This is a statement by a leading agricultural official in Peking.

Only in recent years have bitter experience and severe setbacks convinced the leadership that they should take a practical view of this far from simple state of affairs. At the time of the announcement of the "Great Leap" in 1958, the "simultaneous development" of industry and agriculture by a gigantic and comprehensive effort was still thought possible. 1,000 million Chinese hands were to effect a radical transformation by the judicious deployment of labour under intelligent guidance. The period of the "production battles", the mammoth labour army and the 12- to 14-hour day began. Millions took the field to dull drum beats and shrill gong strokes, made irrigation systems, built dams, shifted billions of cubic feet of earth, smelted iron and steel by "do-it-yourself" methods, built home-made railways on wooden rails, collected manure and destroyed flies and sparrows in mass campaigns. The foundation of people's communes organized on strict military principles was one of the most important features of that new policy. Yet the "Great Leap" was not achieved. Official propaganda, of course, puts the blame for this on the natural catastrophes of the years 1959 to 1961 and the cessation of Soviet economic aid after the open break with Moscow. These events certainly contributed to the aggravation of China's economic distress. However, the decisive factor was probably that the demands put on her capabilities were too great. The development of people's communes met with stubborn resistance among the people. Energy, strength and capital were squandered or else their results bore no relation to the efforts and sacrifices made. Then came a new turn in economic policy. In the spring of 1961 it was decided to give production in agriculture priority again.

From now on the Party's mottoes were: "Walk on two legs", or, "The development of agriculture is the foundation of our national economy, the development of industry its decisive factor." China's economic policy remembered reason and moderation. True, industrialization remains the principal target, but people have realised that the key to its realization is to be found in the reorganization and encouragement of agriculture. Today the results can be observed throughout China. To increase productivity in agriculture, the people's communes were "liberalised"; their number was increased from 26,000 to 74,000 to make possible the introduction of more rational working methods. Not much is left of the original concept of people's communes, which only a few years ago had become the bogeyman of the western bourgeoisie. The communes have been decentralised.

Their actual function today lies more in administration. The tasks of organising labour have been delegated to a lower level. The brigade, that is, as a rule, the village farming community, has become the decisive element; the farmers have been offered increased material incentives. The state purchase price of agricultural products has been raised. At the same time the farmers have been assured that henceforth they will receive more industrial goods in return for their increased income. Most important of all, however, is the return or expansion of the farmers' private farmland. The area for personal use now amounts on the average to about five per cent of the total cultivable area of a people's commune. This measure has not only made the provisioning of rural areas easier, but has also benefited the urban population. Farmers are allowed to sell their own produce to the State or on the open market. Thus, for example, in many regions the sale to the state authorities of pork and eggs from private production amounts to forty per cent of the total state purchases.

We would not be wrong in supposing that the "liberalization" of the people's communes, and especially the concession of individual incentives, have contributed to keeping the general food situation stable, although the level of the production of basic foodstuffs has remained stationary in recent years. For the time being, hunger has been banished from China by the new measures.

The stabilization of agriculture has inevitably produced serious consequences in the industrial field. Admittedly, the development of heavy industry is still the fetish of every Communist official in China. Achievements in this field are demonstrated to the foreign visitor with great pride. But there is obviously a change of objective. It is expressed most clearly by a prominent Chinese economic official: "A few years ago heavy industry was developed with the sole aim of serving heavy industry. Today it is put in the service of agriculture." This change of face has caused a stagnation in China's industrial development that can only be overcome gradually. There was "overinvestment" in the years of the "Great Leap". During the years 1958 to 1960 essential branches of industry supplied the economy with capital goods so quickly and over such a range that industry and agriculture could not usefully absorb them under the existing conditions. The overhasty type of investment policy achieved no results and represented a waste of resources. Today smaller resources are more rationally employed on development. Apart from the armaments industry, which is a closed book to us, heavy industry today is extensively adjusted to the modernization and rationalization of agriculture. Artificial manures, irrigation, mechanization, electrification, improvement of the transport system, those are the Party's industrial slogans nowadays. The production figures for the last few years give a clear picture of the general slowing down of the industrialization programme. Western experts estimate Chinese steel production in 1964 at about 9 million tons. Soviet sources give a figure of 9.5 million tons. In 1958 Chinese steel production had already risen to 11 million tons, in 1959 to 13.35, and in 1960 to as much as 18.5 million tons (excluding the quantities of steel produced by "do-it-yourself" methods). The picture is similar for coal production. With some 220 million tons in 1964, the production position has remained unchanged since 1961. Thus it is considerably below the figures for the years 1958 to 1960. In 1958 alone, for example, 425 million tons of coal are supposed to have been mined in China. With the exception of a few branches of industry immediately important to agriculture, such as chemicals, crude oil, cement or the production of electrical energy, China's present-day industry in general has not yet returned to the 1958 level of development. Not until China's agricultural products appear to be assured on a long-term basis can a start be made on the realization of ambitious industrial plans. So the slogan of agriculture as the foundation of the Chinese economy is certainly not empty talk.

*Progress and problems in the educational system*

Population and economic worries are not the only ones that plague the leadership. It has to face an equally difficult task in the educational system. In 1949 it was estimated that about 90 per cent of the rural population and about 70 per cent of the urban population were unable to read and write. Nine out of ten Chinese at the time were illiterate. Within 15 years these figures have decreased to about 60 per cent illiteracy in the country and 20 per cent in the towns. That is certainly an impressive achievement, but there is still much to be done. The problem of the written language is a special difficulty in primary education. Latinization of the script has proved to be impracticable. Even though the modern characters have been greatly simplified, learning the written language is still a tremendous burden. The expenditure of time and energy is obstructive, but even more so is the inevitable, one-sided development of mnemonic power at the expense of the ability to think logically. The staggering number of schoolchildren is an additional problem. According to official statistics for 1960, 91 million children are supposed to have already attended primary schools in China. Today it is estimated that the 100 million mark has been passed. China was exceptionally short of schools before the Communists seized power.

How were the necessary teaching techniques and personnel to be conjured up with the minimum of delay in order to cope with the mass rush to the primary schools that had quite rightly been encouraged? Wrong decisions in the early years contributed largely to this state of affairs. Very little money was spent on the educational system, and the training of engineers and technicians, not teachers, was given priority. That lesson has been learnt today. Teacher training has been put in the first place, and teaching is by far and away the most popular subject, with about 35 per cent of all students in China. Another handicap emerges in secondary and university education. The dominating, central idea of the regime has always been to educate the growing generation, especially those who are expected to assume leading positions in the future, in accordance with revolutionary and proletarian doctrine.

Because of this, things are unsatisfactory, especially in the universities. The Soviet model of university education, which is mainly aimed at the training of technical specialists with revolutionary political convictions, was widely copied. Only recently have voices been raised in favour of limiting the utilitarian nature of university studies and placing greater value on the standard of scholarship. Political agitation and productive industrial effort have been reduced. These are the first signs of opposition to the dangerous policy of specialization and neglect of fundamental studies. Thus many people in leading scholastic circles have realized that one day a one-sided educational policy in the universities might prove fatal to the development of modern projects in industry and agriculture which called for independent and logical thinking. To solve the dilemma, a new structure is being prepared. In it, conventional institutions retain the purpose for which they were created, while new schools are being founded to train the essential expert industrial and agricultural cadres. In many other spheres also Peking's leadership has become more realistic.

China has recovered from the severe setbacks of the "Great Leap". But the improvements in the basic food situation and the gradually rising production of raw materials and capital goods are still marginal and the successes do not permit of spectacular target setting. For the time being, the leadership has settled for reaching the ultimate goal of China as a modern industrial country by modest routes and on a very long-term basis. The people must be satisfied with the prospect of slow progress.

There is no doubt that the gigantic problems still beset the biggest developing country in the world. But given the diligence, tenacity, pragmatic sense and natural intelligence of the Chinese people, they can look forward to an economic development that might well equal Japan's. To reach that stage will take China many years, perhaps even generations.

*The permanent class struggle*

The Communist leadership in China today seems to be clearer about the arduous and thorny path to the desired goal than most of its fellow-countrymen. It knows about the difficulties and believes that they can only be overcome if a policy of rigorous restraint, iron discipline and ceaseless indoctrination forces people into the paths that seem to those in power to promise success. There are three methods of political control which every visitor to China will find striking. Firstly, there is the organizational ability of the cadres. It reaches with extreme precision into the tiniest villages in the country and into every single family group. Nothing seems to escape the eye of the Party. At mammoth events we see the extraordinary ability of the apparatus to handle human masses just as the initiators had planned in advance, at the same time maintaining uncanny discipline and order.

If a foreign statesman is greeted in Peking, millions form lanes, wave flags, artificial flowers or garlands, roar greetings, make an infernal din with drums and shrill gongs and altogether give an enthusiastic welcome that could leave no one unmoved. If protest demonstrations are organized, the same millions fill the streets in the same perfect order. Instead of the outward signs of welcome, we see clenched fists, posters and banners, which proclaim the demands of those in power in a few pertinent words.

A second aspect of political control is the attempt to exert an all-embracing influence—an attempt that is not deterred by any material sacrifice, effort or expenditure of time. There are political and reading circles in the schools, factories and people's communes throughout the country. Political meetings are held during working hours, in the breaks—even during the pauses in production caused by the occasional breakdown of machine-ry—and naturally in the workers' evening leisure time. For the Chinese citizen political activity and propaganda begin in the kindergarten, accompany him throughout his life and only stop in old age.

Recently a third feature of Communist control has come increasingly to the fore in political training: the cult of Mao Tse-tung. This is not merely an example of the manifestation of power or of the hero-worship of a single figure considered typical of totalitarian systems. In China the cult of Mao Tse-tung is also looked on as a means of helping revolutionary theory to win through. However much Mao Tse-tung the man is praised and glorified, in the next breath the same verbosity is employed to encourage the reading of Mao's works—in other words the people are led from hero-worship to theory. The great importance of fusing man and idea seems to lie in the urgent need to overcome traditional Chinese conceptions of society and its functions, as these were handed down and anchored in the social, moral and political teaching of Confucius for two and a half millennia.

The teaching of Confucius is still alive in China, even though some of it is modified and some of it is unconscious tradition. The leadership is convinced that Confucius must give way to Mao Tse-tung if the heritage which the old combative élite purchased with much blood and sacrifice is to be preserved. The age-old teaching of harmony and balance, of the family and kindred as the foundation of society, the criterion of existence and the sole authority, must be replaced by radical revolutionary Marxist theories.

The gigantic efforts at indoctrination have another purpose: the masses of the Chinese people are not yet by any means as convinced of the expediency of the new order of society as the leadership considers necessary if the desired goals are to be reached. National stimulation and economic organization need a political and ideological foundation among the population.

Anyone who travels through China with his eyes open will find plenty of confirmation of this proposition. On the one hand, the Chinese shows himself willing to follow the slogans blindly. In his excessive zeal, he is not even disturbed by the grotesque contradictions involved. On the other hand, there are just as many signs to make us suspect that the outward show of solidarity has little significance. Obviously, the average Chinese looks on the official version as comfortable protective armour, put on so that he can ward off external influences and quietly follow his own inclinations with as little disturbance as possible. This attitude may be peculiar to the Chinese mentality, which tends to conformity, so we are told. It may correspond to a way of thinking occurring in classical literature, according to which a man only turns to force and open resistance in extreme need, but otherwise strives to overcome his adversary by cunning and deception. It may also be the result of a tradition of denying every authority that lies outside the family. However that may be, this means that the Communist cadres have no real hold on the masses. They blow a note on the trumpet and the right sound comes out. But any deep-seated effect, which is what really concerns the leadership, is lacking. Hundreds of millions of Chinese are like a rubber wall. They make no resistance and comply with the party's directives obediently, but without fanatical enthusiasm. "Slogans, catchwords, campaigns, American imperialism and all the rest of it have little interest for the simple Chinese", I was told by an intelligent East European observer who has been resident in Peking for years. "The only thing that matters to him is whether he has enough rice in his bowl this winter and whether he can buy himself a new pair of trousers next year."

A recent series of measures and propaganda campaigns seems to confirm what the foreigner can observe on a journey through China. The leadership speaks of a permanent class struggle in the country. This battle on the home ideological front, so party officials told me frankly, will last not for a few years, but for many decades. The leadership is afraid that the youth will get soft because, growing up in a peaceful, secure world, they may lose their "vigilance" and show a "desire for an easier life". Hence the call to the younger generation not to lose their "battle-hardened revolutionary dash". The leadership claims that "bourgeois views aimed at falsifying our general line of socialist development" are becoming noticeable among the intellegentsia and must be corrected in a "Great Debate" as Prime Minister Chou En-lai once called it. However, since the end of 1964 the most important and extensive campaign has been directed against tendencies that had appeared in rural districts in threatening numbers. This campaign, carried out by a tremendous number of cadres, is called "*Sse-ching*", the "Four Cleansings". It is aimed against four allegedly widespread phenomena: "corruption in the people's communes", "bourgeois thinking", "reactionary forces" and a "revival of capitalism". These ideologically embellished descriptions, so well-informed sources in Peking assured me, simply concealed a relapse into the customs of the bad old days. In the remoter parts of the country there were presidents of the people's communes who ruled over their domains like notorious warlords of yore. Party secretaries exercised a tyranny of a kind that was customary in the old China. Corruption, smuggling, black marketing and illegal profits from unreported sidelines of the people's communes were the order of the day. Many of those in power locally, so I was told, even had concubines again. The leadership hold that these campaigns, based on the claim that they continue the orthodox revolutionary line and defend the "pure teaching of Marxism-Leninism", are of fundamental practical importance. For unless the "existing opposition in society" and the ideological and political "vestiges" of a traditional view of life are laid aside, China will inevitably relapse into "bourgeois and capitalist" conditions.

In other words, since the premises considered necessary are not yet present in China, the leadership must continue to use harsh uncompromising methods to advance the development they desire. If the reins were slackened too much, the Communist leadership in China is afraid that it might be the end of Communism. The primacy of domestic politics in China is more valid than in any other country in the world. Consequently, when assessing Chinese foreign policy, we must bear the elementary domestic aspects more strongly in mind than has usually been the case in the West. Admittedly, the driving forces of Chinese foreign policy are many and varied. Nationalism, emotionally and historically conditioned anti-imperialism, the natural aspiration as Asia's most populous nation to become the leading power in that continent, the rise in China's prestige, the effects of self-assessment, the ideological break with Moscow making China the sole representative centre of world Communism, these are all independent factors. Nevertheless, the elements of Chinese foreign policy that seem to be decisive are those which must be evaluated as results of the domestic political situation. If the principles of revolution and class struggle hold good in domestic politics, this is equally and inevitably so in the sphere of foreign policy. But, just as criteria of actual power, not dogmatic principles, have the last word in internal affairs, so the sober evaluation of conditions, not militant, ideologically motivated language or aggressive attitudes, is decisive in Peking's foreign policy. This approach, apart from leading articles and bombastic proclamations, has lain at the heart of China's political practice right up to the present day.

# Chungking

重慶

We had planned to travel from Sian to Chungking by the railway that runs west from Sian to Paoki and then to Sinkiang by way of Lanchow. At Paoki, at the western end of the Wei-ho plain, the line branches off south-west. It crosses a spur of Kansu Province and follows the course of the Kialing River in Szechuan Province as far as Chengtu. This connection between Paoki and Chengtu, the capital of Szechuan, was completed in 1957. The journey through the ravines and gorges of this mountainous country is one of the most interesting in the whole Chinese railway system. The trip from Sian to Chungking via Chengtu takes 33 hours.

The evening before our departure, Mr. Pan and Mr. Lin told me we would not be able to travel to Chungking by rail but would have to go by air in order not to miss the connection with the river steamer that was to take us down the Yangtzekiang from Chungking to Wuhan. I was disappointed and annoyed by this news. I had been looking forward to the rail journey from Sian to Chungking for a long time. Travellers who had made the trip in previous years had described it as a unique experience.

The reason, I was told, was that the departure of the steamer had had to be brought forward by one day on account of the unusually strong currents on the Yangtzekiang. This excuse still seems to me to be as incredible today as it did then. I could not help feeling that for some reason I could not fathom, the Chinese authorities wanted to keep us from making the rail journey. Even while I had been in Peking and the special permit was finally granted for the river journey through the Yangtze gorges after long drawn out haggling, we had been told that we would not be allowed to stay long in Chungking, but would have to go aboard the river steamer with the least possible loss of time.

Shortly before noon we took off on the flight from Sian to Chungking. The aircraft rose higher and higher until before long a low cloud layer prevented us from seeing anything. It was not until we were approaching Chungking, two hours later, that we broke through the cloud and got our first glimpse of the Szechuan hills and the rice terraces laid out on their slopes.

At Chungking Airport an official was waiting for us with a car to take us into the town. He told us the steamer would be leaving next morning at 7 a.m.

114/15 *Rice terraces around Chungking, Szechuan.* The road from the airport to the town, 20 miles away, ran along a mountain slope in a series of curves. It was raining heavily, but even so I asked to have the car stopped again and again, so that I could take as many pictures as possible. One pass was covered in thick mist and it became so dark that the driver had to switch on his headlights from time to time. Every now and then spectral shapes would appear out of the mist, hurrying along the road with agile step under their heavy loads, which they carried slung on frames on their backs. We drove down into the valley and came into the first large settlements on the outskirts of Chungking.

116 *Rice farmer with water-buffaloes ploughing near Chungking.* This farmer was wearing a rice-straw cape to keep off the rain. He was making a strange chirruping noise through his teeth to urge the buffalo along. The beast moved ponderously along, step by step, furrow by furrow. I went along the rain-softened and slippery paths (found around every rice field) to get as near as possible to the scene, heedless of the fact that I was continually slipping off the path and that the sticky mud was oozing into my shoes.

The Kuomintang government took Chungking as their capital in 1938, when the Japanese began their conquest of the Chinese eastern coastal regions. This was one of modern China's darkest hours. The Japanese occupied the whole of the eastern half of the country, including the richest and most fruitful provinces. To all intents and purposes Chiang Kai-shek had nothing but the agricultural products of Szechuan Province and the other little-developed nearby provinces. The Nationalists performed many a prodigy of bravery and effort as they moved factories and machines from east to west under appalling difficulties. Universities were set up in small villages and went on working in emergency conditions. But all of this was not enough to enable the Kuomintang to beat the Japanese.

Chungking has a population of over two millions and lies on the sides of a mountain spur that juts out between the Yangtzekiang and Kialing Rivers to the point where the two rivers meet. We drove down to the centre of the city along a broad street. From some distance away we saw a group of people watching parachutists jumping from a training tower, but our escort, who

119

118

wanted to get us to our hotel as soon as possible, hurried us on. I asked him to drive on, saying it would soon be evening and that I should like to go to the place where the Kialingkiang runs into the Yangtzekiang.

117 *Confluence of the Yangtzekiang and Kialingkiang, Chungking.* In the centre of the picture is the Yangtzekiang, down river, looking east, and on the left is the Kialingkiang, which runs into the Yangtzekiang at this point. Groups of men and women carry heavy loads up or down the steep steps that lead down to the river. Chungking is a town of many different levels, and is characterized by steep, narrow alleyways and labyrinth of steps. This is why most goods and supplies have to be carried by porters. Food, coal, building materials and even live pigs have to be laboriously hauled by hand from the river up to the town.

118 *Twelve-man junk on the Yangtze, Chungking.* Navigation on the Yangtze has always demanded great skill and cunning on the part of the helmsman. At this point, where the Kialingkiang and the Yangtze meet, the powerful currents and eddies demand special strength and concentration. Following the commands of the helmsman, the oarsmen plunge their oars into the water in perfect unison and throw themselves back with all their might. As if guided by an invisible hand the clumsy junks glide over the surface of the water.

On the quays there was a scene of busy activity and bustle. Ferryboats came in, disgorging masses of people who had come across from the opposite bank of the river. Goods were being unloaded from little steamers. Tied up alongside the bank were junks that gave one a glimpse of the domestic life of the Yangtze sailors. These spend their whole lives on their junks, the scene of all their activities. Children are born within the hulls of the junks; here festive occasions are celebrated – and here, too, the grim reaper comes to gather in his harvest.

119 *Evening scene on the bank of the Kialingkiang, Chungking.* Dusk is falling over the scene of hurry and bustle and over the junks, on which the Yangtze sailors spend their whole lives, from birth to death. Here and there on the cliff sides, where old houses and wooden huts stand on stilts, the lights begin to go on.

Our escort was becoming increasingly impatient. Finally we drove back through the city in the direction of our hotel. The car drew up before an enormous palace. This was the newly-built People's Hall, to which is attached a modern, two-storey hotel. We were shown into well-appointed rooms, each with a bathroom and a balcony. The food, with the highly peppery seasoning that is the basis of the reputation enjoyed by the local cooks, is of excellent quality and, for the foreigner, remarkably cheap.

There are a surprising number of modern hotels in China. In these hotels cleanliness, honesty and perfect service are the rule. There are at all times smiling "boys" and chambermaids in great number, ready to fulfil one's slightest wish or even to anticipate it. The hotels are standardized but well run, and are in marked contrast to those of former times, when staying in a Chinese hotel was a dark and depressing experience for the foreign traveller. The well-known sinologue Perzynski, neither prejudiced nor particularly sensitive, described his experiences in Chinese inns about fifty years ago in these words:
"In the courtyard of the inn, pigs, hens and dogs play peacefully together, mules are tied up outside the rooms and there are garbage heaps, feet high, in each corner. The 'guest room' is an empty stable, the sky can be seen through the board ceiling, the paper door and windows are torn and unspeakably filthy. My kerosene stove is too small to heat this leaky shed. The other rooms have mud walls and stoves. In these rooms sleep indigent traders or draymen, who feed the stoves with poor Chinese charcoal and wake up rosy-cheeked and cheerful after a truly animal sleep, where we would have been suffocated by the carbon monoxide."
His Chinese fellow-travellers frankly admitted that "even for a Chinese, a night in an inn is a gruelling experience. Europeans are not wanted. They cause too much bother. Recently an innkeeper, who did not even serve tea, was heard to grumble about modern effeteness. Once upon a time, he said, people had been content to sleep all together in one big room. Now only three or four people were willing to share one room. If you travel in summer, nothing will surprise you more than the astuteness of the Chinese bedbugs. They crawl up the walls to the middle of the ceiling and then drop boldly on to your bed."

# Yangtze Gorges

長江三峽

Before daybreak we were already on our way to the lower part of Chungking. A great number of steps led down to the pier. We lugged our considerable baggage down the steps from one level to another and thrust our way through the crowds. It was some time before we discovered from a ship's officer that we were on the wrong pier: the "Chang-ling", the Yangtze steamer we were making for, was lying at another on the opposite side of the town! Panting and dripping with sweat we hauled our baggage up the steps again, to find that by good fortune our car was still there. We drove with breakneck speed to the other end of the town and thus managed to reach the steamer, out of breath and the last passengers to go aboard immediately before the steamer cast off.

To the accompaniment of blaring music from the ship's loudspeakers we joined the other passengers at the rail to observe the manœuvering of the ship and the departure from Chungking. Very soon the steamer was passing the last of the Chungking factories and after a few curves and bends we found ourselves in the midst of wonderful river scenery.

Our first-class cabin was right forward on the top deck, so that the thudding of the engines was hardly noticeable. We laid out our things in the cabin. The journey from Chungking to Wuhan is 800 miles long, and we would be spending three full days on board the steamer.

120 *Yangtzekiang between Chungking and Changshow, Szechuan Province.* A few hours after leaving Chungking we reached a part of the Yangtzekiang that is notorious for the many reefs in the middle of the river. The ledge of rocks in the bed of the river, often enough below the surface of the water, depending on the prevailing level of the river, are one of the things that make navigation on the Yangtze so difficult. The dangerous spots are well marked, however, and the captains of the river steamers can pass through the deeper parts without trouble.

121 *On the Yangtzekiang, Changshow.* The river steamer made short calls at various points to pick up or land passengers and freight.
As the steamer approached one of these places, the captain would give a blast on the siren to warn both the crew and those on land to prepare for mooring.

The siren also mobilized a great number of fruit sellers, who would gather at the landing stage or surround the steamer in their junks.

122 *Fruit sellers alongside the "Chang-ling".* The fruit was handed up to the passengers on the upper deck in little baskets on long poles. Most of the passengers, however, took the opportunity to go ashore and buy their fruit there.

123 *Yangtze steamer near Fuling.* Just before reaching Fuling we met the "Chang-ling's" sister ship sailing upriver. Going upstream, the steamers take almost twice as long to cover the same distance because of the strength of the current in the upper reaches and particularly in the famous Yangtze gorges.

Our steamer, the "Chang-ling", has a displacement of 2,300 tons and is fitted with two 2,400 h. p. diesel engines. The ship, 210 feet long and with a 45 feet beam, draws 7-9 feet of water. She was built in the Kiang-nan shipyard in Shanghai. The crew of 75 were trained in the School of Navigation in Wuhan. The "Chang-ling" has four decks and 606 sleeping berths in various classes. In a pinch she can take up to 1,000 passengers, but in that case any surplus passengers travelling fifth class would have to be content to sleep where they could on the floor.

124 *The quay at Fuling on the Yangtzekiang.* On the first day of our trip down the river we called at Changshow, Fuling, Fengtu, Kaochiachang and Chunghsien. Meanwhile, dusk fell and it was soon pitch dark. The markings to guide the ships' navigators are excellent, even at night. Projecting cliffs are denoted on the right bank by red lights and on the left bank by green lights, enabling the helmsman to take the ship safely between them.

Towards nine in the evening we reached Wanhsien, where the steamer tied up and stayed overnight. Like the other passengers, we took advantage of the opportunity to go ashore. We climbed a number of steps to the level of the town. Hawkers were stationed along the edge of the street offering their wares, which included large numbers of suitcases, arranged neatly in piles. We wandered through the dimly-lit streets and bought fruit.
In a small eating-house lit by a single bulb, people were sitting on narrow

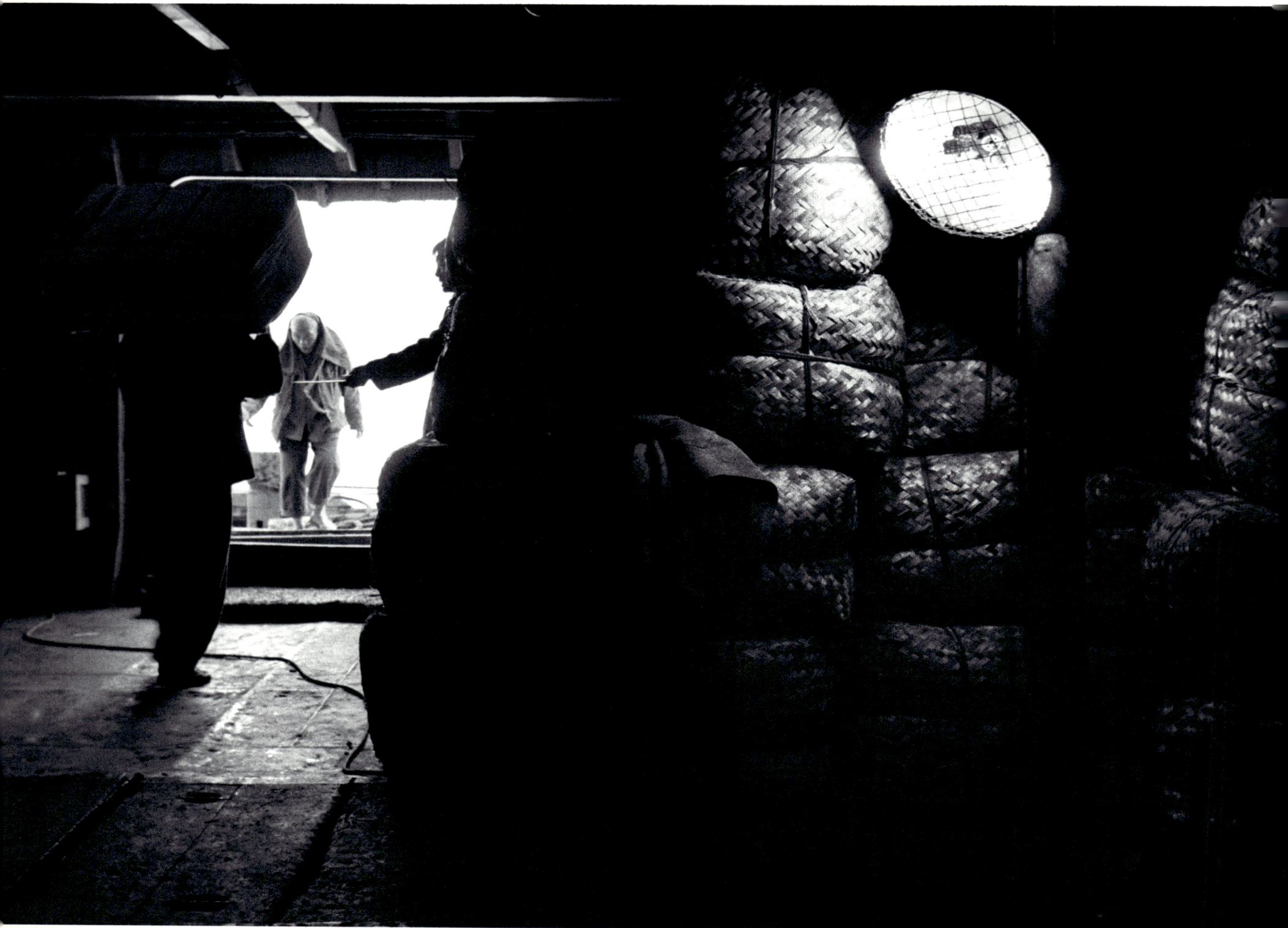

126

127

benches at plain wooden tables. We went in and joined them and they offered us something to drink. Foreigners are very rarely seen here and we were at first the object of curious attention, but after a while the conversations were resumed, with much laughter and joking. The place was filled with the steam from a small cooking range in the corner.

On the way back to the ship I took a flash picture of a small food stall. The owner, who had not seen me, came bounding out, gazed at the night sky and muttered some incomprehensible words before going back to his counter with much shaking of the head. He was obviously wondering how there could possibly be a thunderstorm at this time of year, with only one flash of lightning and no thunder at all.

At 6 o'clock the next morning the ship's siren jerked us out of our sleep. The "Chang-ling" was weighing anchor, ready to continue the journey down the Yangtze. Immediately next door to our cabin was the first-class saloon, with a wide window giving a fine view. Grey clouds were hanging low over the water, but the weather outlook seemed a little more encouraging. At least it had stopped raining.

125  *Peasant houses on the south bank of the Yangtzekiang near Fengchieh.* The settlements on the river banks are built high up so that they will not be imperilled by high water. The natural high-water mark is shown by a clear line running along the bank. At certain points, particularly in the narrow gorges, heavy rainfall after a long period of drought can make the Yangtzekiang rise as much as ninety feet in a few hours.

126  *Water-level marks on the Yangtzekiang.* The water levels are shown at intervals in the more dangerous parts of the river. The boat-towers, who have to tow their craft against the stream at certain points, have a difficult time of it. Where the cliffs are particularly steep, narrow towpaths are cut into the cliff face.

127  *Unloading from the "Chang-ling".* Freight is unloaded or taken on at the various stopping places. The porters carry the bales on their shoulders to the freight store and receive from the foreman a small bamboo tally for each load: and are paid according to the number of tallies they produce.

The mountainous country of Szechuan produces a variety of commodities, including medicinal herbs, tung oil, wax and gall-nuts. Even in pre-Christian times Szechuan's remarkable natural wealth and its pleasant climate made it known in popular parlance as "the heavenly land". It was the many streams and rivers which gave it its name, *sze chuan* — "the four rivers".

The Yangtzekiang is 3,600 miles long, making it the longest river in China. Its catchment area covers half a million square miles, equivalent to a fifth of the area of the whole of China. It rises in the mountainous frontier territory of West Tsinghai and Tibet. The upper reaches wind through West Szechuan, East Tibet and Yunnan and the central reaches through the Red Basin. Then it breaks through the Wu Mountains in three gorges on the border of Szechuan and Hupei and flows over the vast plains through Hupei and Anhwei Provinces, finally running into the East China Sea in Kiangsu Province.

Even in earliest times communications and transport between the East and Szechuan ran through the Yangtze valley and the three gorges. This waterway, running through deep gorges and past craggy cliffs and numerous sandbanks, and always in an unbridled torrent, was in the highest degree difficult and dangerous. "The way to Szechuan is hard, harder than the road up to Heaven", wrote Li Po, the great poet of the T'ang Dynasty. It is the difficulties of communication that have led to the economic development of Szechuan Province lagging behind.

Since time immemorial important communication routes have led via the Yangtzekiang into Szechuan and the two great outer regions of the Chinese empire, Tibet and Sinkiang. Today no foreigner is permitted to visit these provinces—and there seem to be good reasons for the ban.

Tibet, taken by the Chinese in 1950 after the "great northern snow country" had declared its independence following the fall of the Manchu Dynasty, has never found peace even to this day. In 1959 there was a bloody revolt against the Chinese occupying forces and the primate of the Tibetan theocracy. The Dalai Lama had to flee to India. There have been repeated reports of partisan activities by the rebellious Khampa tribe, who regard the Chinese as interlopers and are doing their utmost to thwart Peking's efforts to turn their country into a Chinese land. There does not seem to have been much change in the unhappy situation even now that Peking has formally acknowledged Tibet to be an autonomous region of the Chinese People's Republic. The basic fact remains that the Chinese leaders have the country firmly in their hands.

In Sinkiang, too, the political situation in many areas is reported to be far from calm. In the course of the Sino-Soviet conflict both the Soviet and Chinese press have published reports on troubles and clashes in the frontier regions. These are probably mainly ethnic in origin and are a continuation of troubles created by the membership of nomadic tribes living on both sides of the frontier, the Mohammedan Uigur and Kazakh minorities. This may be the cause of the occasional friction between the Chinese authorities and the local inhabitants.

However, the real reason why Sinkiang is barred to foreigners is probably that the southern portion of the area is the proving ground for Chinese atomic research. It was here, in the Takla Makan desert, that the Chinese exploded their first atom bomb. The authorities in Peking are unlikely to want to allow foreigners sight of their Central Asiatic experimental area or to let them see what is going on on the transport routes to the place.

Around noon on the second day of our voyage we approached the first of the three celebrated Yangtze gorges, which together have a length of 130 miles. The first one is five miles long and is called "Chu-tang-hsia" or "The Bellows". Here, as Mr. Chen Che-chia, the 30-year-old First Officer of the "Chang-ling", told us, a ship had been wrecked in 1945. Towards the end of the war, Japanese bombers were penetrating as far as the eastern regions of Szechuan and forcing the Chinese to confine the movements of their larger ships to the hours of darkness. The "Chi-ling", which was sailing upriver during the night, hit a projecting cliff shortly after leaving the first gorge and was smashed to pieces.

128  *Going through the "Wu-hsia", the second Yangtze gorge.* The second gorge, "Wu-hsia" or "Witches' Gorge", is 45 miles long. In places the river is less than 150 yards wide and the "Chang-ling" had to keep close in to the steep cliff face. This second gorge is said to be the place where, in 1949, shortly after the

Revolution, the steamer "Feng-tu", loaded with fuel for Chungking, was blown up by Kuomintang secret agents, killing 45 of the crew of 50.

129  *In the "Hsihing-hsia", the third Yangtze gorge.* The "Hsihing-hsia" or "Gorge of the Western Grave", is the longest of the gorges, being 75 miles long. The journey through the rugged mountain scenery in the gathering dusk was particularly impressive. We occasionally met junks, which can hoist their sails when the wind is favourable.

130  *Freight steamer in the third Yangtze gorge.* We overtook this freighter before dusk fell, and soon afterwards we were sailing through the last part of the third gorge in complete darkness. The "Chang-ling's" searchlights lit up the steep overhangs in ghostly fashion as we sailed on through the night between the green and red marker lights. The journey through the pitch dark gorges, past overhanging cliffs that reflected the sound of the ship's siren in eerie echoes, was an experience never to be forgotten.

131  *Small passenger on board the "Chang-ling".* We stopped for a short while in the dark at Ichang, the first town after the gorges, and then went on. Soon after the evening meal there was not a passenger to be seen on deck, and they all appeared to have gone to bed. At 9 p.m. exactly the loudspeakers played us the "International" as a lullaby.

By the morning of the third day we found ourselves in completely different surroundings; the "Chang-ling" had by now covered a considerable distance through the great Hupei Plain. The Yangtzekiang, with its enormous catchment area nourishing 250 million people, a third of the Chinese nation, well deserves the name of "Father of Rivers". This king of Asiatic rivers has often enough demonstrated its might. From 246 B.C., when the first records were kept, to 1948 it had overflowed its banks 979 times. The high water mark in the catastrophic floods of 1931 stood at six feet, the highest in living memory. In that year the streets of Hankow could only be traversed by boat. But in the 1954 floods the highest water mark stood at eleven feet. The town of Wuhan was only saved from utter destruction by the superhuman combined efforts of hundreds of thousands of people. To this day, more than ten years

135

134

later, the saving of Hankow ranks as a modern Chinese epic. Three hundred thousand men and women streamed out into the nearby Shen Mountains with bamboo yokes and, working day and night, carried earth to the breaches in the river wall to shore up the embankments and danger points. Many a heroic individual deed has been immortalized in word and picture, deeds of single men and women who sacrificed their lives for the sake of all. A new national epic has grown out of the gallant sacrifice of the people who, when the river was tearing breaches in the dykes, stood tightly-packed shoulder to shoulder in the howling gale, holding back the pounding waters with their bodies while the holes were sealed up behind them.

132/33 *The Yangtzekiang near the great Tung-ting-hu Lake.* Now the banks can only be seen as a thin line: the Yangtze seems to have turned into a sea. We did not stop anywhere on the third day. The nearer we got to the river's lower reaches, the denser the water traffic grew, as freight ships and junks moved up and down the river.

Towards evening we approached our destination, the industrial centre of Wuhan. Not far from the Yangtze Bridge we passed the spot where Mao Tse-tung swam the 1,100 yards across the river at 70 years of age.

134/35 *The Yangtze Bridge, Wuhan.* The building of the Yangtze Bridge took from September 1955 until October 1957, and employed the service of 2,000 workers to deal with the 30,000 tons of iron and steel and the 50,000 tons of cement. The distance between the two main supports is 1,100 yards and the total length of the bridge is 1,670 yards. The height of the supports overall was given to us as 240 feet. The average clearance allows ships up to several thousand tons to pass, even during periods of high water.
The bridge has two storeys, the lower one taking a double-track railway line and the upper one for cars and pedestrians. Although the traffic is very meagre, it is strictly forbidden to stop one's car on the bridge even for a second. The Yangtze Bridge is the first and, at present, the only bridge in the central and lower reaches, and creates for the first time in the history of China a means of direct communication between North and South China. The eyes of the residents of Wuhan light up with pride as they speak of "their" bridge.

# Wuhan

武漢

Wuhan, the capital of Hupei Province, has a population of two millions. It was created in 1927 by the amalgamation of the three towns of Wuchang, Hanyang and Hankow. Wuchang, the oldest settlement, lies opposite the point where the Han Ho flows into the Yangtzekiang. Between the Han Ho and the Yangtzekiang lies Hanyang and on the opposite bank, liable to high-water flooding, lies Hankow with its docks. Unlike Wuchang, which has retained its Chinese character, Hankow, under foreign influence, has taken on the appearance of a European commercial city.

136 *View of Hanyang on the bank of the Han Ho*. Wuhan has developed rapidly since 1949. On the south side of the Yangtze, on terrain safe against floods, there has grown up a centre of heavy industry, the Wuhan iron and steel combine, with machine tool factories that can produce lathes up to 480 tons, vertical and horizontal milling-machines to handle objects up to 25 feet in diameter, and grinding and stamping machines.

137 *The entrance to the Wuhan Iron and Steel Combine*. When we visited the Wuhan Iron and Steel Works the entrance was decorated with a red archway to mark the Chinese National Day on 1st October, The works were built with Soviet assistance, the first two blast furnaces being fired in 1958. The works employ 70,000 workers, of whom 30,000 are building workers engaged on the construction of new installations.
Chinese engineers told us that the sudden withdrawal of the Soviet specialists in the summer of 1960 had caused the combine considerable damage. At the very time when Soviet expert help was most needed, that is to say as the plant was about to go into full production, the Chinese were left in the lurch. The Chinese engineers were inexperienced and they lacked technical skill and know-how. They could not deal with the problems that continually arise in connection with a complicated system. The result was the loss or at least a fall in production. Every branch of production was affected, the ore preparation, the steel manufacture and particularly the rolling mill.
It was planned that sheet metal was to be produced in Wuhan by the end of 1960, and this was the basis of the agreement. But even today only the naked concrete housing for the metal-rolling plant stands in the vast factory grounds. Only now can the Chinese begin to think about completing the

rolling mill, as Chinese industry is now able to produce the necessary components without outside help.

The industrial centre lies about 20 miles from the centre of Wuhan. A housing estate has been built around it to accommodate 240,000 people, who travel between the factories, their homes and the town in motor buses and trolley buses.

138 *Open-hearth furnaces in the Wuhan Iron and Steel Works*. An engineer is measuring the temperature of the steel in one of the furnaces with a modern measuring instrument. The production target of the Wuhan Iron and Steel works is 1.5 million tons of pig-iron and more than 1.5 million tons of steel. All our attempts to get information on the present state of production were in vain. We were frankly told that no figures are given to foreigners.

139 *Art students in the Wuhan Iron and Steel Works*. From a catwalk running along above the open-hearth furnaces I saw several steel workers who had joined a group during a work break. One or two of the group were sitting on stools, with sketch blocks in front of them sketching the workers. We scrambled down the next available ladder and went over to the group, who had not noticed us up to that point. The workers turned out to be students of a Wuhan art school. They were a little put out at our appearance and, feeling inhibited by our presence, they closed their sketch blocks and prepared to go. Through the interpreter I explained that they should not let themselves be put off. I told them that I myself had originally been an artist and illustrator, that I had attended art schools in Switzerland and Paris years before and had not changed over to photography until later. The students, all likeable young men, were touched by fellow-feeling and soon went on with their work. A glance or two at their sketch blocks showed me that some of them had real talent. The blinding crimson glow of the furnaces, just being tapped, provided a wonderful background. As we were about to go a short while later, one of the students came up to me, thrust his sketch block and pencil into my hand and made signs indicating that I should draw something. Now, of course, it was my turn to feel inhibited, but I could not back out, even though it had been 25 years since I had last drawn from life.

I could not tell whether it was the heat of the nearby furnace or the effect of the dozens of pairs of eyes gazing at my sketch block that brought me out in a sweat. I tried to do a quick sketch of a steel worker standing near me and then handed him the result. This was not the end, however. He handed the block back to me and asked me to sign the sketch. The outsize signature I scrawled across the page caused a burst of hearty laughter. I took the opportunity to shake hands all round and depart.

140 *Workers in the Wuhan Iron and Steel Works*. Just before we ended our tour of the steel works we met a group of workers coming off shift. They stood around in their overalls and safety helmets, laughing and joking and wiping the sweat from their foreheads. In spite of the eight hours of solid work they had just finished they showed little sign of fatigue or discontent. They seemed to believe in what they were doing and to be proud of "their" steel works. In front of the main gate there was a queue of female steelworkers. They were carrying small children, whom they had collected from the factory crèche before catching the trolley-bus home.

The "Wuhan Meat Processing Factory" is the biggest slaughterhouse in Hupei Province. Designed by Russian experts and built with Russian help, it was opened in 1958. A visit to this well-run and impressive plant is one of the standard items on the tour programmes for foreign visitors.
As we arrived in front of the building a large number of pigs were being driven in through the gate. We followed them into the interior of the slaughterhouse. A ramp led to the fifth floor and it was an amazing thing to see and hear the squealing and recalcitrant porkers scrambling up the ramp and round the bend to the first intermediate floor. We were of course shown to the lift and ascended ahead of the pigs.
However, we did not have to wait until they arrived from below, as some of the previous herd were still on the fifth floor. After the pigs had been put through a hot bath they were driven into a square enclosure surrounded by a low wall. Within the enclosure were men armed with what looked like electric earphones. These men tried to apply the humane-killers behind the ears of the pigs, which were making a deafening din and kicking out wildly, in order to give them the death-dealing shock. The dead pigs were grasped

by strong hands, hung up by their hind legs from a guide rail and pushed, still palpitating, to the next processing stage.

141 *In the Wuhan Slaughterhouse*. At a later stage the carcases suspended from the guide rail are cut down the middle by an electric saw in a matter of seconds, and the sundered carcases are divided into their separate parts in different sections of the fifth floor.
Another traveller to China, who had paid a visit to this slaughterhouse the previous year, had told me that the management had been planning to set up a special department to process the gelatine produced in the slaughterhouse into photographic film. But when we asked whether they had started producing the film, the embarrassed reply was that it had been decided not to proceed with the scheme. It had emerged that producing film would involve too many problems for the plant, so the gelatine would continue to be sent to a film manufacturing plant in Shanghai. What a pity! I would have liked to replenish my rapidly dwindling stock of films with new rolls marked, "Made in the Wuhan Meat Processing Factory".
Six thousand pigs were slaughtered on that day. I am by no means a vegetarian and enjoy a well-prepared filet and a glass of good wine. But I had never before been in a slaughterhouse in all my travels on various continents. My visit to the Wuhan slaughterhouse was enough to satisfy me for all time.

# Changsha—Shaoshan

韶 山

Shortly after leaving Wuhan, the train bearing us southwards slowed down to cross the great Yangtze Bridge. Just before the train mounted the bridge there was an announcement about the bridge over the loudspeakers and this was followed by the playing of the Chinese national anthem. The train crossed the bridge slowly and then resumed its journey to Changsha, the capital of Hunan.

The area south of the Yangtze, and especially the regions of the Great Lakes, Tung-ting-hu and Poyang-hu, are mainly devoted to rice-growing. The sheer extent of Hunan's rice cultivation cannot be appreciated from the ground: one must fly over the area to get a view of the apparently limitless rice plantations in this region, which is one of the food-surplus areas of China.

142 *Air photograph of rice fields in South Hunan*. This photograph was taken in 1934 by Count Wulf Diether zu Castell. An extract from his notes at the time described the floods in those years:

"The Peking-Canton route was flown for the first time in the summer of 1934, with stops in Chengchow, Hankow and Changsha. At the end of July the level of the Yangtzekiang began to show a menacing rise. It had been raining for weeks and even though the embankments had been considerably raised since the great 1931 floods cost hundreds of thousands of lives, there was a great danger that if the rain went on, there would be another catastrophe. Two weeks later the water level in Hankow had reached that of 1931 and as it continued to rain without ceasing the river waters went on rising. In the country-side the dykes broke and soon Hankow was an island in the middle of an expanse of lakes stretching for a hundred miles. Our landing ground in Hankow was fifteen feet below the water level. If one of the dykes near to us had broken, the tremendous force of the rushing water would have destroyed the whole town. In view of the imminence of this possibility, no aircraft were left on the airfield overnight. But we could still land at Hankow, which we could not do at Changsha, for the airfield there had been under water for weeks and the ground was so soft that it was no longer safe to land on. A road rather like a dyke led from the town to the airfield and this served for landing and taking off, but it was difficult to turn round at the end of the dyke because it was so narrow and every time we did turn round we were in danger of plunging into the fields below.

"We tried to keep at least the mail service going. The mail for Changsha was simply thrown out of the aircraft and the outgoing mail was hung on a double line strung over a couple of posts. We would then fly low over this to pick up the mail-bag with a hook we trailed behind us."

We drove by car from Changsha to Shaoshan, the birthplace of Mao Tse-tung, about 60 miles south-west of Changsha. After we had gone through the town of Siangtan, we came to hilly country, passing sturdy farmhouses lying on wooded slopes among the rice fields. We were assured on all sides that the rice harvest being gathered in in the south at this time was a very good one.

143 *Rice harvest in Shaoshan, Mao Tse-tung's birthplace*. The rice stalks are cut in bundles in the fields and then threshed against the inner side of the basket-like container until the grains fall into the container.

Shaoshan, a small peasant settlement with some 2,000 inhabitants, lies in a valley surrounded by wooded hills. This is a place of pilgrimage for many Chinese, as we saw from the line of motor buses and lorries standing before the "reception" building. The local innkeeper took us along a narrow path by the side of a brook into a small neighbouring valley. After a short climb we reached a small farm. The farmhouse had clearly been restored and had newly plastered walls and new tiles. This was Mao Tse-tung's birthplace. Mao Tse-tung was not brought up in conditions of poverty. The house, though simple and sparsely furnished, has four living rooms and bedrooms and a large kitchen. There are stalls for cattle at the back of the farmyard. There is no lack of agricultural implements and household tools. The Mao family possessed 22 *mo* (about three and a half acres) of rice fields and a vegetable garden and some woodland. At all events the family's land holding was large enough to allow Mao's father to engage extra hands, especially at harvest time.

144 *Mao Tse-tung's bedroom in the Mao family house, Shaoshan*. As a boy Mao had a bedroom of his own, which also served as his study. He was already reading subversive and revolutionary literature, although he had to keep it secret. For this reason he used to cover the window of his room at night. Books such

144

143

147

148

as Shen Shih's "Words of Warning", which Mao read despite his father's ban, had a great influence on him.

145  *The entrance hall of Mao's birthplace.*

Mao spent the first sixteen years of his life in the home of his parents, where he was born in 1893. To judge by the remarks of our guide, Mao must have been a paragon of a boy and his family's life must have been marked by abiding affection and harmony. But according to Mao's own biography, as he related it to Edgar Snow in 1936, his youth was characterized by a continual state of fitful, angry revolt against his tyrannical father. Mao Tse-tung's father sold about half his rice for cash and kept his dependents on frugal but adequate rations. Once a month he gave the hired labourers eggs with their rice, "but never meat", said Mao. "To me he gave neither eggs nor meat."
The old man regularly beat his children to secure unquestioning compliance. He was himself barely literate enough to keep books, but he sent his sons to school, hoping to see them become good businessmen and help him "amass a fortune".
Mao's mother was wholly illiterate and a devout Buddhist who gave young Mao religious instruction. "She was a kind woman, generous and sympathetic. She pitied the poor and often gave them rice when they came to ask for it during famines. But she could not do so when my father was present. He disapproved of charity."
"When I was thirteen I discovered a powerful argument of my own for debating with my father on his own ground, by quoting the classics. My father's favourite accusations against me were unfilial conduct and laziness. I quoted, in exchange, passages from the classics saying that the elder must be kind and affectionate. Against his charge that I was lazy I used in rebuttal that older people should do more work than younger, that he was over three times as old as myself, and therefore should do more work."
When Mao was about thirteen his father invited many guests to their home. A dispute arose between them and the old man denounced Mao before everybody, calling him "lazy and useless". Infuriated, Mao cursed him and left the house, threatening to commit suicide. His mother ran after him and begged Mao to return.

"My father also pursued me, cursing me at the same time he commanded me to come back. He insisted that I *k'ou-t'ou* (knock head to earth) as a sign of submission. I agreed to give a one-knee *k'ou-t'ou* if he would promise not to beat me. Thus the war ended and from it I learned that when I defended my rights (dignity) by open rebellion my father relented but when I remained meek and submissive he only cursed and beat me the more."

146  *The kitchen of the Mao Tsai-sui family in Shaoshan.* Not far from the birthplace of Mao Tse-tung, we paid a visit to the Mao Tsai-sui family, whose small farm we reached by narrow paths running around the rice fields. Cheng Hsi-ling, the mother of the family of six, was busy in the kitchen at the large stove of the type found all over this area (and in Mao Tse-tung's birthplace). They said they were not related to Mao Tse-tung's family and that there were many families in Shaoshan with the name of Mao.
Our visit took the farmer and his family by surprise. No foreigner had ever before entered his house, in which Mao Tsai-sui's grandfather had lived. The mother brought hot water and we sat on narrow wooden benches around the table and sipped it Chinese style while they told us about the projected great "Shaoshan irrigation system". In Hunan Province alone there are to be 100 miles of canals, and 7 tunnels and 19 aqueducts are to be constructed.

147  *Women using a treadmill to irrigate fields.* For the irrigation of the rice fields, the water is collected in ponds and led to the fields from ditches, brooks and canals by means of ingeniously constructed water wheels. Although modern China has many mechanical and electrical pumping stations, it will be a long time before humans are no longer to be seen on the treadmill.

148  *Geese on a road in South China.* In the country districts, far from the hustle and bustle of the towns, the traveller can still come across scenes testifying to the traditional Chinese art of "living slowly and enjoying without haste". The Chinese work hard, certainly, but they also possess the gift of enjoying that quiet happiness that is in such sharp contrast to the hectic lust for life, outwardly rich but often inwardly hollow, of many other peoples possessing more advanced civilizations.

# Kweilin

桂林

I had been particularly interested in this area for many years and had collected much information about it. Even while I was preparing for my trip to China I knew that I should have to exert every effort if I was to be able to visit the Kweilin region and take pictures of the unique landscape for inclusion in this book. It was, in fact, only after protracted and wearying discussions that the authorities in Peking could be persuaded to give me special permission to visit Kweilin.

From Changsha the Peking-Canton Express took us still further south, past the Heng-shan mountain range, the southernmost point of the five sacred mountains. We changed at Hengyang and arrived in Kweilin after another twelve hours in the train.

The journey from Hengyang took us deeper into the eroded landscape so typical of the provinces of Kwangsi, Kweichow and Yunnan. In these provinces masses of limestone extend for hundreds of miles; their area of 230,000 square miles puts them among the largest in the world. Very high summer temperatures and massive rainfall have eroded the mountains to the point where the sole remaining evidence of the strata that once covered this vast area is the remarkable rock formations towering above the plain, often rising to a height of hundreds of feet.

Poets were already celebrating this landscape as far back as the Sung Dynasty. The domes, towers and cones of decaying chalk and the bizarre shapes of the mountains are typical of Chinese landscape painting.

We were met at the Kweilin railway station by Mr. Lun Yi, who took us to a small inn near a little lake, away from the city centre. This house, presumably once the property of a Kuomintang military officer or senior government official, was reserved exclusively for us. I could not tell whether this was deliberately done in order to keep us in isolation, or whether the Chinese thought that the hotel in the town, which we had passed on the way to the house, did not come up to the standard expected by Western travellers.

Travellers in China are continually speculating on the motives and reasons behind the Chinese refusal to allow foreigners to visit certain areas. One reason may be the authorities' obsession with the idea that the visitor must never be allowed to go short of anything, so that they will not grant a travel permit unless the area concerned has good hotels and capable interpreters.

More important, however, are the obviously political reasons for banning visits to certain provinces and localities or refusing to allow foreigners to go to areas which, as was officially hinted to us, are not accessible because of "poor economic conditions".

That evening I asked to have a car for 5 a.m. the following morning, as I wanted to climb one of the three imposing eminences inside the town. We reached the summit, climbing the steep steps cut out of the rock, before the sun was up.

149 *Sunrise from the peak of Tien-sai-shan, Kweilin.* Below us the town is gradually coming to life. I have set up my tripod and camera with telephoto lens, aimed at the brightest spot above the hills in the east, where soon afterwards the sun comes up as a brilliant disc in the cloudless sky. A few residents of Kweilin, wooed from their beds by the wonderful weather and the promise of a glorious sunrise, have also gathered on the narrow summit of Tien-sai-shan.

150 *View from Tien-sai-shan of part of Kweilin.* Two towering rocks, Fu-po-shan and Tu-shu-shan, stand as if on guard over this part of the town. Kweilin was founded during the T'ang Dynasty. In 1943, during the Sino-Japanese war, the Japanese set fire to the town. The holocaust raged for four days and nights, reducing 99 per cent of all the houses to ashes. But today Kweilin, with a population of 230,000, has factories making electrical goods, motor car spare parts and textile and agricultural machinery.

151 *Fishermen using cormorants on the Likiang, Kweilin.* The fishermen propel themselves along on narrow bamboo rafts while the cormorants dive for fish. The birds' necks have been tied up so that they cannot swallow any but small fish, and they are trained to bring back to the rafts the fish they catch. The fishermen take the fish from the cormorants and throw them into large baskets.

152 *Main street in Kweilin.*

Rice is grown in the Kwangsi plains but it is not possible to develop plantations of any size because of the towers, hills and mountain ranges and also

152

153

because the humus layer in these inhospitable limestone regions is too shallow. Moreover, the limestone is full of cracks and holes and cannot store sufficient water. This makes it difficult to irrigate the fields and hinders agricultural development in general.

153 *Winnowing rice in a Rice Brigade near Kweilin.* The threshed rice grains are brought in from the fields in baskets and spread out on clean ground in the drying-yard to dry in the sun. When the grains are dry the rice is tipped into a winnowing mill. This is driven by hand and produces a blast of air sufficient to separate the husks from the grains.

It was here in the south that we came across one of the Chinese People's Republic's special problems, that of the minorities. The provinces of the south are the home of a considerable number of different races. According to a census taken in 1958, seven million of the twenty million inhabitants of Kwangsi alone were of the Chuang tribe. But there are also others, such as the Hsiao, the Mulao and the Tung. They have their own style of dress and in their physical characteristics, facial features and general bearing they resemble the peoples of the neighbouring lands on the other side of the frontier more than Chinese. Most of them live in inaccessible areas in the vast jungles covering the mountains. They were the original inhabitants of this part of China, who were gradually driven into the mountains by the advancing Chinese over the centuries.

The mountain peoples and the Chinese have distrusted and disliked each other ever since. The original inhabitants regarded the Chinese as interlopers, while the Chinese regarded the queer little people as barbarians. There was little intermarriage, each race keeping itself to itself, the Chinese mostly staying in the few towns and on the plains and the minorities in the mountains or in the jungle.

It was only recently, with the advent of the Kuomintang era, that any attempt was made to draw the mountain peoples into the official Chinese state organization. The Communists continued the process. A complicated system of autonomous regions and districts was introduced. The Chinese were careful to allow for the national feelings of the minorities and to give them their own status in administrative and cultural affairs. For example, the majority of key positions on the administrative councils of the autonomous regions are held by members of the minorities, even when the Chinese population is very much larger. "It is their homeland, after all", we were told time and again. On the other hand, the Chinese have also been careful so to lay out the autonomous regions that the minorities can never make themselves independent or break out of the great national framework. One method is the breaking up into a number of autonomous regions of any compact areas with a large non-Chinese population. There are, for example, ten separate Tibetan districts. In the autonomous regions of the Muslim Ninghsia Hui there are estimated to be a million Chinese as against 600,000 Hui. The remaining half-million Hui, although they live in the same area, belong to Kansu Province, where they form an insignificant minority.

The Chinese are pursuing a similar policy in the south. Presumably the minorities in South China foster their national traditions and desire to keep alive their own way of life: but it cannot be denied that the Communists have done great and beneficial work in this area. Only a decade or two ago Western journalists and missionaries were bringing back reports of unbelievable conditions in this part of Asia. Crime, opium-smuggling, child-labour in the primitive tin-mines, slavery and slave traffic were all quite common. In the interior, the rice trade and commercial traffic were menaced by bandits, and anyone who wanted to traverse the region with a caravan had first to hire an armed body-guard if he wanted to be reasonably sure of getting through. Life may be less colourful, exotic and exciting today, but for the great mass of the people, Communist rule has brought order into their daily existence, an existence that may be poor and shabby but is at least better than it was before.

# Kweilin–Likiang–Yangsuo

漓 江

Our guide wanted us to spend another two days in Kweilin. There were, he said, so many beauty spots to see in the town that even three days would not suffice to see them all. What was more, we had not inspected one single factory. But this failed to move me. I was not prepared to waste a single hour touring a factory while I was in the midst of this glorious scenery. So that evening I demanded some serious discussion. I pulled out my notebook with the details of this region that I had been getting together for years and pointed out that while Kweilin was a very interesting place, I happened to know that the loveliest scenery was to be encountered further downriver, at Hsingping and Yangsuo. Mr. Yun was taken aback. Then I quoted to him the centuries-old Chinese proverb saying that the landscape around Kweilin was exceedingly beautiful but that the landscape on the Likiang far outdid it in loveliness.

My suggestion, therefore, was that we should find a junk by the next day and make the trip down the Likiang from Kweilin to Yangsuo, which would take us two days. Mr. Yun, visibly shaken by this, objected that it was already dark and too late to organize a boat and crew for the next morning. I tried to win him round by remarking that we did not want to make this trip only for our own pleasure, but that it would be to the benefit of Kweilin — and China — if my book contained pictures taken in the Likiang.

And Mr. Yun managed it. That very night he found a boat, rounded up a crew and arranged for provisions. Early that morning clean bedding was put aboard and by 7 a.m. we were pushing off.

The crew consisted of three strong men to man the oars, a cook and a steward. I complimented Mr. Yun on his extraordinary performance. I could well imagine the strenuous efforts he had had to make in order to make this trip possible. We noticed at once that the crew had even reported aboard in new clothes and new rubber shoes.

The three oarsmen poled the junk out into the middle of the river with long bamboo poles. We had only covered a mile or so of our voyage when the steward, to our surprise, brought us hot tea and biscuits.

154   *Children crossing the Likiang on a bamboo raft.*

Our speed varied between one and six miles an hour, depending on whether we were in calm water or rapids. I was particularly happy to be at last on some vehicle that did not have vibrations to make my work difficult. The lovely weather made us all feel in a good mood.

155   *A group of cormorant fishermen on the Likiang.* These fishermen and their cormorants are very common on the Likiang. At this point they have used nets to enclose part of the river. Here the cormorants dive for the fish and take their catch to the fishermen on the rafts.

156   *Water-wheels on the Likiang.*

157   *Group towing their boat up the Likiang.* We met a number of boats travelling upstream. In a strong headwind or in places with a very rapid current, several members of the crew would go ashore and haul the boat upstream at the end of a long rope.

158/59   *Settlement on the east bank of the Likiang.* We sailed past a number of small hamlets lying on the banks of the river. These places cannot be reached by road and even inside them there are no streets to speak of, so that the whole of the village activity takes place on the river bank and all movement is by water. This circumstance enabled us to get many a glimpse into the life of the settlement and the junks moored up alongside the banks.

160   *Scene on the Likiang between Kweilin and Yangsuo.*

A thousand years ago the poet Han Yu said of the Likiang, "The river is like a lady's belt, the mountains like an azure jade hair-stick". When the wind dies down and the grotesque shapes of the mountains are reflected in the water, one could fancy oneself in an enchanted scene. The only ones who do not feel the magic are our poor oarsmen, who have to row the whole time.

As dusk fell we moored up somewhere along the river bank and dropped anchor. Covers were put up all round, mattresses spread on the deck and the whole area converted into a bedroom for us all.

157

158

161 *Sunrise over the mountains on the Likiang.* Early next morning we set off again. Shortly afterwards the first rays of the sun flashed over the huge black domes of the hills, which were reflected in the waters of the Likiang.

On the previous evening our Chinese escorts had been talking about the famous "Long March" of the Red Army. At the end of the 1920s, Mao Tse-tung had founded a soviet republic in the quiet shelter of the mountains of the border area between Hunan and Kiangsi, gathered together the remnants of the Communist Party that Chiang Kai-shek had smashed in the towns and built up a partisan army largely recruited from the peasants of these remote regions. Chiang Kai-shek pressed the revolutionaries hard. In the autumn of 1934 the pressure of the Nationalist Chinese was becoming so intense that Mao Tse-tung decided to retreat. In twelve months, under continuous pursuit by the Kuomintang troops, Mao's men covered over 6,000 miles from the far south, through East Tibet to Yenan in Shensi Province not far from the Gobi Desert. When they left Kiangsi in the autumn of 1934 the main force of the Red Army numbered 90,000. Of these, only 7,000 reached the new headquarters in Yenan. They had been 368 days on the way: their average daily march was 18 miles. Almost every day they had been involved in skirmishes with the enemy and sometimes in open warfare.
In order to keep contact with the enemy to a minimum, the march had led through trackless wastes, through regions in which hostile Chinese tribes had resisted them, through disease-ridden jungles, swamps in which hundreds of them sank without trace, through icy mountain passes where many plunged to their deaths. Provisions were of the scantiest and the shortage of water was even worse. "Sometimes our people were obliged to drink their own urine", Mao has related.
The situation became particularly critical when rivers had to be crossed against opposition. The Red Army crossed 24 rivers, most of them representing not only natural obstacles but also a vital link in the enemy's defence line.

One of the first dramatic events in the "Long March" took place north-west of Kweilin at the crossing of the Wukiang. This is described in the following extract from the account written by Air Marshal Lin Ya-lu:

"The battle for the Wukiang crossing opened on 1st January 1935. At this point the river is 250 yards wide and the current is extremely strong. The southern approach to the river was a cliff road three miles long leading downwards along the steep slope. On the northern bank there was also a long path to climb to reach the highway to Tsunyi and Tungtse. The enemy was busy digging trenches on the other side of the river and did not notice our arrival. Keng Piao, the commander of the leading regiment, disguised himself as a peasant and went to the bank to spy out the lie of the land. On the opposite bank, about 500 yards upstream, a narrow path wound its way to the road leading to the ferry. This path, a key position for the enemy defence, was almost impassable. A landing would be difficult because there was no jetty. The enemy had posted sentries and erected defensive ramparts 100 yards away. A thousand yards back from the bank, in a temple, reserves in regimental strength were available, and half way up the hill, a mile and a half from the river, the main body was stationed, also in regimental strength.
"It was decided to mount a fake diversionary attack on the road to the ferry and to concentrate the main attack on the narrow path leading upriver. We immediately sent bridge-building material down to the ferry to draw the enemy's attention to it.
"As expected, the enemy immediately stopped work on their defences and opened fire. Pioneers quickly put together bamboo rafts. Eighteen good swimmers were selected and given the job of swimming over the river, disposing of the enemy sentries on the river bank and providing cover for the crossing by the main force.
"At 9 a.m. on 2nd January the fake diversionary attack began. The enemy troops hastily jumped into their trenches and opened fire on the south bank. At the same time, however, our troops started the main attack. The first eight men, armed with Mauser rifles, jumped into the river under cover of fire from our machine-guns and trench mortars, reached the other bank in about ten minutes and concealed themselves under the cliffs held by the enemy. The first raft was sunk by enemy fire. The eight men who had already landed on the other bank could do nothing without reinforcements, so they were recalled. The first attempt to cross the Wukiang had failed. It was now decided to try the crossing in the dark.
"That evening the 1st Battalion of the 4th Regiment assembled at the edge of

the river. All was quiet, with only occasional shots to be heard. Five men boarded the first raft. It had been agreed that as soon as they reached the opposite bank, they would give a signal by flashing a torch. The attack on the enemy sentries would not begin until a complete platoon had got across safely.

"The second raft was boarded by the company commander, Mao Cheng-hua, with a runner and three machine-gunners. The third and fourth rafts were to follow once the second group had landed.

"Twenty minutes had gone by since the first raft had pushed off, but there had been no torch signal, so the third and fourth rafts were held back. An hour later the five men on the first raft came back. The current was too strong; they had lost their direction in the dark and, despite all their efforts, they had been swept down river. We had to assume that the second raft with Mao Chung-hua aboard had also been carried away. It was therefore decided to carry out the crossing in daylight after all.

"Following two days of skirmishes, the enemy called up reinforcements in regimental strength. On the third day, at 9 a.m., another diversionary attack was launched on the ferry. 500 yards upstream twelve men on three rafts reached the opposite bank under heavy covering fire. The second group started. The enemy was firing continuously at the rafts, when suddenly, underneath the cliffs on which the enemy had posted his sentries, several men appeared as if from nowhere, opened machine-gun fire on the nearest enemy troops, hurled hand grenades at them, causing them heavy losses, took the position and gave covering fire to the landing of the three rafts.

"Who were these men? They were the company commander, Mao Cheng-hua, and his men, who had reached the south bank that night after all. But as they were too near to the enemy and no raft had followed them up, they had not dared to send us the torch signal. Unnoticed by the enemy they had held out ever since, directly under their position.

"As our vanguard moved up the hill along the narrow path, three regiments of enemy reserves arrived. The path was the only way up and the enemy troops wanted it for the counter-attack. But our heavy fire barred the way. As the hill was very steep and the path very narrow, our vanguard were stopped half way up and suffered heavy losses from the enemy's fire. Our men found another place among the steep cliffs that could be climbed and

managed to take the enemy's key position on the summit. Meanwhile a company of our troops had already got across the river, took the other positions and destroyed the fleeing enemy."

It was not only in the case of the Wukiang but also in the later and extremely difficult crossings of the "Golden Sand" River and the Tatu in West Szechuan that the Red Army managed again and again to achieve their objective with skill and cunning, even though they suffered heavy losses.

The exciting story of the "Long March" has become a legend in modern China. Here was a group of determined and fanatical revolutionaries who, by the exercise of unexampled moral and political willpower in what was by all normal standards a hopeless situation, achieved the impossible. The self-same leaders who survived the "Long March" have been in power in China right up to today. Their thoughts and actions bear the stamp of the experiences of that dramatic epoch.

On the second day, our junk made good progress. A breeze sprang up, not very strong but enough to allow us to hoist the sails. Our crew, who had been rowing without pause up to this point, could at last have a rest.

162 *Junks on the Likiang.* Boats have come up aft of us. Thanks to their larger sails, they soon overtake us and leave us behind.

163 *Water buffalo crossing the Likiang.* This farmer was taking his buffalo across the river. From the middle of the river onwards the water gets deeper and the buffalo and his rider had to swim the last part of the way.

Before us lie some rapids, which increase our speed considerably. But our helmsman takes the boat skilfully through them. Ahead of us we can see more rapids, through which a junk is making its painful way.

164 *Mother and daughter towing a boat against Likiang rapids.* These two had to exert every last ounce of strength, clutching at rocks wherever possible and straining with their whole bodies to get the boat through the rapids.

165 *Group towing a boat on the bank of the Likiang.* One person always stays aboard to manage the steering. If the boat belongs to a small family, it is often the grandmother who takes over the rudder while the younger ones go ashore and haul on the rope.

166/67 *Junks on the Likiang.* If there are a number of people on board, only part of the group goes ashore to haul the boat upstream at the end of the towrope. The others stay on board, their part being to push with long poles. Starting at the bow, they press the end of the pole against the river bed, fit their shoulder into the curved crook at the end of the pole and thrust with all their might, pushing the boat along until they reach the stern. Then they return to the bow and repeat the process.

Towards evening a fresh headwind blew up. Our oarsmen had to pull their hardest to make sure we reached our destination, Yangsuo, on time. Here a car was waiting to take us back to Kweilin, while our junk turned about and began the return journey upstream. We had made the 40-mile trip downstream in two days, but they would need six or seven days for the journey back, depending on the wind.

The final stage of our travels took us from Kweilin to Hengyang, Canton and then to Hong Kong for the flight back to the west. What we had seen on the Likiang, the hard life of the junk-sailors amid the unforgettable beauty of the scenery, had made an impression on us that would not soon fade from memory. The life of these people seemed directly symbolic of a nation struggling to master its fate under the most arduous conditions, a nation that despite all hardship and affliction has lost neither courage nor hope nor its proverbial light-hearted cheerfulness.

# Acknowledgments

The present book of photographs would not have been produced without the kind help of the Chinese authorities. I am especially grateful to Mrs. Kung Peng, who for many years has been in charge of the whole press and information service in the Ministry for Foreign Affairs, with the title of Assistant Minister. Not only did she show interest in this project, but also understanding of wishes that could not be so easily complied with in China as elsewhere. I offer my sincere thanks to the Head of the Information and Press Service of the Federal Political Department in Berne, Mr. Walter Jaeggi, and I feel deeply indebted to the Swiss Ambassador, Mr. Hans Keller, and his wife, as well as Mr. Arnold Hugentobler, Mr. Walter Wild and the other hospitable members of our Embassy in Peking, who assisted me in every possible way. During my preparations for the trip, I received help and information from Wulf Diether Graf zu Castell, Munich; Professor Dr. Heini Hediger, Zurich; Professor Johannes Schubert, Leipzig; Professor Robert P. Kramers, Zurich; Dr. h. c. Henri Dumur, Wetzlar; Willi Petraglio, Biel; Albert R. Diener and Fritz Girardin, Swissair Zurich; Adolf Faes, Zurich; Ernst Debrunner, Zurich; Adolf Lemans, Zurich; Ingrid Parge, Zurich; Ruth Naegeli, Zurich; Hans Frei, Zurich, and Fritz Hofer, Zurich.

I thank Professor Dr. Emil Egli, Zurich, Edgar Snow, Nyon, and Harry Hamm, Bonn, for their contributions to the text. The text by Edgar Snow contains extracts from his book *"The Other Side of the River"*, Random House, New York; Victor Gollancz Ltd., London; Editions Stock, Paris; Kindler Verlag, Munich, which he revised and enlarged specially for this photographic book. I owe special thanks to Harry Hamm, who edited my account of my travels and contributed valuable additions. Some extracts from his book *Das Reich der 700 Millionen* were included in my travel narrative by kind permission of Econ Verlag, Dusseldorf. The Chinese names and geographical descriptions in the text are generally adapted to the English Wade-Giles transliteration.

The tireless work of the management of the photogravure firm of Imago, Zurich, and the specialists employed on the photogravure printing ensured that my book of photographs was faultlessly produced. Ernst Gerbig, with whom I checked the colour proofs, contributed decisively to the faithful colour of the reproductions by his gift of sympathetic understanding.

Forch-Zurich, Autumn 1966                                          Emil Schulthess

# List of Illustrations